A COSMIC
ENCOUNTER

About the Author

Stewart W. Bench (Upstate New York) is a retired electrical engineer who experienced several encounters and abductions. Thanks to his engineering background, Stewart has been able to describe the technical details of the alien entities, spacecraft, and technological equipment, including his own implant.

A COSMIC ENCOUNTER

A TRUE STORY OF AN ALIEN ABDUCTION

STEWART W. BENCH

LLEWELLYN PUBLICATIONS
WOODBURY, MINNESOTA

First Edition
First Printing, 2021

Book design by Samantha Peterson
Cover design by Shira Atakpu
Interior art on pages 28, 37, 39 and 180 by Llewellyn art department
    based on art provided by author
Interior art on pages 113, 124, 131 and 182 provided by the author

Llewellyn Publications is a registered trademark of Llewellyn Worldwide Ltd.

Library of Congress Cataloging-in-Publication Data
Names: Bench, Stewart W., author.
Title: A cosmic encounter : a true story of an alien abduction / Stewart W.
    Bench.
Description: First edition. | Woodbury, Minnesota : Llewellyn Publications,
    [2021] | Summary: "For the first time, Stewart Bench tells the
    incredible true story of being encountered and then abducted by aliens.
    As an engineer, Stewart uses his technical experience to describe the
    specifications of the alien craft, their technology, their
    communications, and their mission"—Provided by publisher.
Identifiers: LCCN 2021022083 (print) | LCCN 2021022084 (ebook) | ISBN
    9780738769509 (paperback) | ISBN 9780738770062 (ebook)
Subjects: LCSH: Bench, Stewart W. | Alien abduction—United States. |
    Human-alien encounters—United States. | Electrical engineers—United
    States—Biography.
Classification: LCC BF2050 .B45 2021 (print) | LCC BF2050 (ebook) | DDC
    001.9420973—dc23
LC record available at https://lccn.loc.gov/2021022083
LC ebook record available at https://lccn.loc.gov/2021022084

Llewellyn Worldwide Ltd. does not participate in, endorse, or have any authority or responsibility concerning private business transactions between our authors and the public.
    All mail addressed to the author is forwarded but the publisher cannot, unless specifically instructed by the author, give out an address or phone number.
    Any internet references contained in this work are current at publication time, but the publisher cannot guarantee that a specific location will continue to be maintained. Please refer to the publisher's website for links to authors' websites and other sources.

Llewellyn Publications
A Division of Llewellyn Worldwide Ltd.
2143 Wooddale Drive
Woodbury, MN 55125-2989
www.llewellyn.com

Printed in the United States of America

To B: my love, my partner,
my mentor, and my critic.

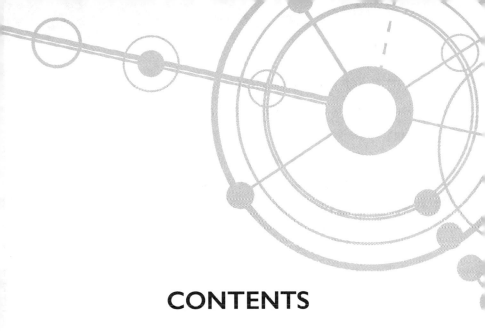

CONTENTS

PART TWO: OBSERVATIONS

INTRODUCTION

This is the story of my life-altering encounter with extraterrestrial beings. The intent is to provide the reader with a highly absorbing and entertaining narrative that offers an unprecedented wealth of information on the aliens and their technology.

The extraordinary episode began in the early 1990s, just before the TV series *The X-Files* popularized the concept of alien visitation. Contemporary literature, which I had for years enthusiastically devoured, presented accounts of human contact with aliens that quite typically offered only vague details or bizarre and often preposterous assertions. This paradigm provided a fulcrum from which to assess the extraordinary insight granted me into the cosmic visitors' physiology and their remarkable technology. What I discovered regarding the aliens and their ship was documented at the time in the rigorous regimen instilled in graduate engineers. Likewise, the information was filtered and colored by the prism of that training as well. What resulted was a record of observation and explanation, and on occasion conjecture and theory, propounded from an engineer's perspective.

Many years following the encounter, the realization dawned on me that I was in possession of a plethora of information that is unparalleled in typical books and the media. This led to the decision to advance public awareness by publishing this account, which the reader will hopefully find to be both fascinating and informative.

This book is organized into two parts. The first describes my three meetings with the extraterrestrials and cites what were at first numerous rewarding consequences. The ominous and devastating turn that events later took for me and my family is revealed in a number of chilling anecdotes. Part two offers extraordinary insight into the aliens and their technology. The aliens' mission and their physical and mental makeup are discussed in detail. The structure and operation of their spaceship is also extensively explored in areas such as propulsion, navigation and life-support systems, failsafe and protection methods, crew quarters, and more. Included at the end of the second section is a discussion prompted by research into what I perceive to be a few popular myths connected with extraterrestrials.

To avoid the possibility of annoying repetition, the terms "alien," "Gray," and "extraterrestrial" are used interchangeably throughout this narrative.

Part One
ENCOUNTER

chapter one
SMALL TOWN BOY

When other kids were fascinated with pterodactyls and tyrannosaurs, I was captivated by the admittedly primitive movies and comics of the late 1950s and early '60s that depicted rocket ships, Venusians, and Martians.

During summer vacation from elementary school, my friends and I would drag home large cardboard boxes tossed out as trash by the local appliance store. These made great rocket ships for youngsters with keen imaginations. We'd search the garage and cellar for stuff that we could visualize as belonging in a spaceship. Adding to our imagined realism were an old radio chassis, a large electric motor, a defunct window fan, and a cardboard control panel with a few real electrical switches attached and dials and knobs drawn on it in crayon. We'd seat ourselves on folding chairs in front of a window cut in the box and take off for distant worlds on an afternoon's adventure. In a few days, the weather would do in our creation, and one of the dads would fold up the soggy mess and toss it in the trash. There was always another rocket ship waiting at the Square Deal Supply.

As a teenager, I developed a strong interest in the country's achievements in space exploration and in particular the Apollo program's manned missions to the moon. As a young adult, I would scour science periodicals for articles on the NASA probes and relished the fantastic photos of the planets and moons transmitted from afar.

I was certain that the popular imagery of green, gray, humanoid, and reptilian aliens portrayed in the stuff I was reading was fantasy. My conception of a *real* extraterrestrial life-form had been that of an amoeba squirming its way through the ooze at the bottom of a lake on an otherwise barren place a few hundred light-years from here. That changed abruptly in 1977 with the release of Spielberg's *Close Encounters of the Third Kind*. For the first time, it dawned on me that extraterrestrial life could actually be a race of intelligent bipedal beings.

My horizon expanded markedly with the launch of the Hubble space telescope in 1990. Clearly visible in the stunning photographs returned to Earth were colorful interstellar gas clouds and billions of stars, many presumably with planets—some that might even harbor life.

I began to devour whatever I could find on the subject of aliens, human abductions, animal dismemberment, crop circles, UFO sightings and crashes, lights in the sky, the small airborne spheres called orbs, you name it. Although thoroughly fascinating, it was obvious that a lot of it was out-and-out fiction. Still, I continued my reading, relishing those tomes I considered authentic, knowing that this material was the closest acquaintance I'd ever have with this subject that so enthralled me.

The rest of my history, up to a point, was fairly mundane. I was born in 1952 in upstate New York and attended a centralized school in my hometown. Following high school graduation in 1970, I went on to receive an electrical engineering degree from a state university. A month or so after graduation I interviewed for a position as a staff engineer in a newly minted small electronics firm located an hour's drive (in good weather) from home and began a forty-two-year career there.

I knew my future wife in high school. Bev and I dated off and on for a number of years, interrupted by the four years we both attended college. We were married in 1975 and moved into a tiny rented apartment for a few years. We were both employed and eventually secured a loan to buy a home on a small lot in our hometown. Our son, Ted, was born in 1976 and his sister, Ann, was born in 1978.

Ours was a comfortable and rewarding existence. We experienced the typical family triumphs and disappointments, joys and sorrows, laughter and tears for the first seventeen years of our marriage. And then things changed.

chapter two
RED SQUIRRELS

In the late spring and early summer of 1992, we experienced a population explosion of red squirrels. Adults and at least one litter of baby squirrels had taken up residence in our snowmobile shed and a smaller nearby tool shed. Aside from their voracious appetite (they ate more than their share of the generous supply of black oil sunflower seed in our bird feeders), they are notorious for chewing stuff that shouldn't be chewed; electrical wiring, for example. The little buggers managed to gnaw an entry hole in an aluminum vent on the tool shed.

It became imperative (a wifely decree) to do something to reduce the squirrel population. Doing them in wasn't an option; I'm too much of a pacifist. So, a live capture trap was purchased, and a trapping campaign was undertaken. Attracted to a gob of peanut butter that we smeared on the trap's trigger platform, we began to have success capturing the critters.

Relocation of the captured squirrels was a sticky issue. In some regions such a thing is frowned upon by the authorities. Not being certain about local restrictions in this still predominately farming area of the state, and not wishing to get an official ruling that might result in a much less palatable solution, we elected to go ahead with the repatriation endeavor. Pivotal in the effort was finding a location where the newcomers wouldn't be likely to interact with human habitation. In this we are particularly fortunate in our region because there are large expanses of out-of-the-way roadways adjoining pastureland and wooded areas with widely separated homesteads and farms.

We found an ideal spot within a few miles of home. I had already made a number of relocation trips to this unpopulated spot, believing that keeping the squirrel families together was the humane thing to do. One particular late afternoon trip on an unusually hot day in late August was to be fateful.

Having dropped off the fifth or sixth squirrel, I turned the truck around and headed homeward. A half mile or so from the drop-off point, I glanced at the mirror and observed what appeared to be a single headlight on a vehicle a fair distance behind me. Believing it was probably a motorcycle (as unlikely as that would be on this particular roadway), I initially gave it little thought. I was doing around fifty miles per hour, and it was obvious that the motorcycle was gaining on me. It occurred to me that the rider was going much too fast for the uneven rocky and dusty surface of what we call in these parts a dirt road. Before long, it became apparent that the light, now very bright and almost filling the rearview mirror, was not a part of something on the roadway; it was attached to something above the road. I began to slow the truck as the view in the mirror took the form of a metallic saucer-shaped vehicle hovering a few yards above the surface.

At this point, things began to happen in quick succession. First, the FM radio station I was listening to became garbled, then noisy, and then the radio became quiet. Shortly thereafter, the truck's engine began to misfire. I pulled off to the side of the road, turned off the engine (it probably would have died on its own at that point), and found that the truck was engulfed in shade on what was a bright sunny day and in an area without a tree in sight. It was stone-quiet except for occasional metallic creaking of the truck body. The truck was vibrating slightly at a low and inaudible frequency.

Frankly, scared poopless (or more precisely, closer to the other extreme), I considered the few options available to me. Stay in the truck, which was obviously under some sort of extraordinary external influence, or bale out, hoping to make a getaway. The first and most reasonable thing to do was to see if the engine would start. It turned over and fired intermittently but wouldn't continue to run. With the engine malfunctioning, and the air conditioner inoperative, the prospect of hanging around in the truck on such an unusually hot day was unappealing.

I decided to leave the truck. At this point a bit of curiosity overcame me as well. Just what was this thing that had somehow disabled the engine and was hovering over my truck, causing this huge area of shade? I opened the door and stepped out. In retrospect, that was an unwise move. I immediately became aware of a tingling sensation on my unprotected skin and the feeling of being exposed to intense sunshine even though the sun was shaded by the object. My discomfort was soon forgotten at the amazing sight I was witnessing.

Wow! I had read many descriptions of alien spacecraft and had seen many blurry, nondescript photos of them. It constantly perplexed me that with the proliferation of video and still cameras no decent pictures of one had ever been published. Well, I sure didn't need a picture; there was one now floating seventy-five feet or so over my head. It was a gray metallic color and was shaped very much like two deep dessert plates, one inverted on top of the other, stuck together at the rims; indeed, the familiar description of a flying saucer. There was a bulbous protrusion with what appeared to be observation ports mounted topside. This feature wasn't visible from my position at the time, in that it was eclipsed by the mass of the ship due to the sight angle. I observed the dome later as the craft departed. I estimate the dimensions of the craft to have been thirty feet or so in diameter and fifteen feet at its maximum height excluding the top part that added another three feet or more in height.

Having breathtakingly discovered the source of the shade engulfing the truck, and the electric or magnetic field that was causing the truck to vibrate, I decided the best course of action was to put as much distance as possible between myself and that spaceship. Not so easily done, as it turned out.

As I briskly walked away from the saucer and my truck, which it obviously still had in its clutches, my heart sank as I turned to look back at the craft. It had begun to move and was following me as I trotted along the road. The saucer soon overtook me and sped ahead, descending to a few feet above the roadway, blocking my retreat in that direction. *Two can play this game.* I abruptly turned and hurriedly marched off in the opposite direction. Again, the ship quickly overtook me again and hovered a few feet from the road surface a few yards ahead of me. *Okay, they've got me. Now what?*

As I stood there, honestly quaking in my boots, three struts emerged from the bottom of the craft and appeared to lock in place. The ship then quietly descended until supported on the struts. After a minute or so, a panel, roughly four feet in height, opened in the side of the craft, leaving a rectangular aperture that revealed a dimly illuminated interior. A ramp then deployed from the bottom of the port and continued its extension until it contacted the surface of the road.

As I watched in near panic, a dark form briefly obscured the light visible in the opening. A person, or more appropriately, an entity, then emerged from the craft. The being's appearance conformed in many respects to familiar descriptions I'd read of aliens popularly known as Grays. The first entity was soon joined by a second who could have been his twin in that they looked exactly alike to me. Both were about four feet tall (they had to duck when coming out of the craft) and were roughly humanoid in appearance. They were profoundly skinny and had proportionally oversized heads. They wore what appeared to be gray and somewhat glossy suits or uniforms covering all but their head, and surprising to me, they didn't wear a helmet or have a respirator or any other obvious form of a life-support system. Their facial features, except for their large dark eyes, were diminutive: a tiny slit that could roughly pass for a mouth, two small orifices where a nonexistent nose would be, and two indentations where one would expect to find ears. The aliens' very thin arms were comparatively much longer than ours, and their hands had three long thin fingers and a thumb. Their feet were covered in extensions of their suit or possibly boots, I couldn't be sure, and appeared to be appropriately shaped and sized for their body proportions.

One of the two Grays was staring intently at me. Suddenly a calm feeling overtook me. The anxiety and fear that had troubled me simply melted away. I equate the feeling to the effect of taking a strong tranquilizer except in this instance the result was immediate.

The second alien then turned and reentered the ship. A few moments later he reemerged carrying a few items.

The second alien approached me, and before I could react, grabbed a lock of my hair, sliced it off with a sharp-edged knife-like instrument, and dropped it into a small container that he then handed to the other Gray. *What the hell!* I thought. Even in my alien-induced serenity I was totally bummed out. These guys had snipped off a lock of my hair without so much as a warning. But that was nothing compared to what happened next.

The first Gray then grabbed my right hand and turned it palm upward. I considered resisting, but then thought better of it. The second Gray then extended my middle finger and poked it with a sharp cylindrical instrument, taking a chunk of skin and flesh about a sixteenth of an inch in diameter. *Damn, that hurt! What's with these guys?* The Gray then dropped the instrument into another container and produced a vile of a viscous liquid that he dabbed on the hole in my finger. The pain immediately subsided and the bleeding stopped.

Then what could very roughly be considered a conversation began between the aliens and me. The Grays didn't speak. As I came to find out, they only communicate telepathically among themselves and also with humans, where they convey ideas, concepts, suggestions, and ethereal images that manifest in the mind of the receiving party. The process does not require either participant to possess a spoken language. At least in the case of alien/human exchange, the process is remarkably imprecise. The aliens rely on constant feedback to ensure that what they've communicated is really being understood. It can take many iterations of back-and-forth mental dialogue to nail down the essence of an exchange.

Apparently the Grays are able to mask their own communication from human interception. They had to be talking to each other the whole time, but I was left out of the conversation. Much of what I was able to discern from the aliens' attempts at reaching me was vague at best and getting to that level of understanding was an effort. Considering that telepathic communication was totally new to me, I surmised that they were probably having as much trouble understanding me. And, what I most urgently wanted to convey and have them fully understand was *Leave me the hell alone*. At first, I was uncertain as to which entity I was communicating with. It eventually dawned on me it was the one staring at me. Although thought transfer can occur without the need for eye-to-eye contact, I learned later that the technique greatly improves the clarity of the received thought impressions.

I was telepathically given the notion that I was important to these guys, that they were on a mission of exploration, that I was a potential subject, and a determination would be made later as to whether I was a suitable candidate. Depending on their subsequent evaluation, I might or might not ever see them again. I preferred the latter possibility.

There was a lot I wanted to know. *Why me?* And if I was selected for whatever they had in mind, how would I know? And, if I was chosen, just what would that entail? Would I be probed, prodded, skewered, and sliced? Considering events of the past few minutes, the prospect was not promising. The Grays were totally unresponsive to my inquiries. Maybe they didn't feel the need to satisfy my curiosity. Then again, as a rank novice in the art of telepathy, maybe they just didn't understand.

The entire incident to that point must have taken less than an hour. I suddenly got the impression that I was now free to leave, and I couldn't take them up on it fast enough. I felt the very strong compulsion to return to the truck, and specifically to close any open windows. The two aliens abruptly turned, entered the waiting saucer, the ramp soon retracted, and the access port suddenly sealed without the slightest indication of a seam.

I sat in the truck waiting to see what might occur next. I knew it was unlikely that I'd be able to start the truck until the UFO left. After a few minutes, the craft slowly and silently lifted off the road and the struts retracted into the body of the saucer, leaving no indication whatsoever of any panels or openings from which they deployed. The bright light that I had seen initially, and which it occurred to me had been extinguished during the visit, came on in dazzling intensity, and the craft shot straight up, tilted slightly, and was gone in an instant.

I was profoundly glad that I had adhered to the very strong compulsion to enter the truck and close the windows during the departure. I was already feeling sunburned on my face and arms from exposure to the saucer. The truck's key was dangling in the ignition switch, which was off, but as the craft arose, the interior lights of the vehicle came on spontaneously, glowing softly; static and a low rumble sound emitted from the radio speaker. Even inside the vehicle, the hair on my arms tingled and my meticulously combed and slicked down hair stood on end. I wondered as the craft disappeared if my truck was toast. Being a techno-geek, I owned an early bulky analog cell phone commonly called a bag phone; it was home connected to its charger. Calling a garage to arrange for a tow was out of the question. The walk to the nearest house would be tough in the summer heat, and it could be a long wait for another vehicle to happen along.

The radio came on when I turned the key, the truck started normally and, greatly relieved, I headed for home shaken by what had transpired and very glad it was over. It occurred to me how ironic it was to feel the terror and excitement I had experienced contrasted with my detached, unsympathetic reaction when reading about a similar encounter involving someone else.

When I arrived home, in leaving the truck, I noticed that the paint color on the hood and top of the cab was now a darker red than the sides. So be it, my compelling need at this point was for a couple of beers and a few moments of solitude in my lounge chair. Of course, the family inquired how come it took me so long to deliver that squirrel and what I'd been doing to get that sunburn. I made up some lame excuse, something like I'd stopped to assist an older gentleman change a tire and was rewarded with a beer or two at a bar afterward. I wasn't about to disclose the events of the day to anyone … not yet anyway. I reserved the right to ponder on my own timetable what had happened to me in an attempt to reconcile it with my normally mundane lifestyle.

The squirrels got a reprieve. I decided that five or six transplants were enough. The ones remaining were welcome to the birdseed. I was not about to travel to that isolated area again. I'd just have to come up with a reasonable excuse for abandoning the eradication program.

A few weeks later, with my finger long since healed and my unusually severe sunburn finally transformed into a deep tan, I had become convinced that my encounter was a one-time thing. I no longer cared about or even noticed the discolored paint on the truck, and the memory of the incident began to fade. I was happy to dismiss the whole affair. In time, I thought, I might eventually feel like talking about this bizarre situation with a few empathetic friends and family members. Then again, they'd probably think I had been high on something or, worse, that I was crazy. It was all behind me now and I was none the worse for the episode.

chapter three
CLOSE ENCOUNTER OF ANOTHER KIND

Fall and winter passed without event, or at least without an alien-inspired incident. We endured the usual allotment of snow and daydreamed as we did every year about a time when we might be able to escape the frigid north and spend a couple of months somewhere warm. Maybe next year.

I used what free time wasn't spent with a snow shovel or roof rake to read my latest acquisition of an extraterrestrial tome. By late March we had survived yet another winter and the last of the snowbanks left by the plow finally melted away toward the end of April.

Time passed. By late spring of 1993, the grass was growing like mad, but the lawn wasn't getting the attention it deserved.

We were having a particularly rough patch at work. We had taken on a fixed price contract to design and deliver a large power supply unit, and the very aggressive delivery date was looming. We had produced a prototype that had major problems and the engineering staff (myself included) were burning the midnight oil trying to get the thing to work right. The effort meant lots of unpaid overtime and the sacrifice of every weekend for over a month. Routine homeowner tasks suffered as a result.

Late one Friday evening, I arose from my slumber to visit the bathroom as I typically did about halfway through the night. On this occasion, it occurred to me that the moon was unusually bright that evening. The trees and bushes were clearly illuminated in a bluish white light as I idly peered out the window on the way to my destination. It didn't occur to me until later that it was dark outside as I returned to bed after my less-than-two-minutes bathroom stop. In referring to the calendar, I discovered that the moon wasn't going to be full again for weeks. I was at a loss to explain what I had observed the night before; I'd probably been dreaming.

The next morning, I woke up with a strong compulsion to blow off work that Saturday and maybe Sunday too. I contemplated a much needed getaway. I wasn't even going to call in; they'd just have to get along without me for one weekend. I recalled that my friend Jim owned a camp located on an isolated lake just outside of the Adirondack Park where our families had occasionally gathered for summer swimming and barbecuing. Jim had often said that we were welcome to use the camp anytime it was vacant. It was an appealing offer, but we hadn't exercised the option. I decided that this was an opportune time to take him up on it. A phone call confirmed that I would be welcome, where to find the key, and how to light the cabin's temperamental gas fireplace. The trip would involve a few hours' drive and that, too, would be a stress-relieving occasion. The family understood; they acknowledged that I very much needed this time to myself. So, with the latest purchase of an alien encounter book that I found so interesting and that often distressed me as well, and with a stop at the grocery store for food essentials (bread, sandwich meat, cookies, and a six-pack of beer), I started out for Jim's camp. I intended to stay the night and return home early Sunday morning.

It was a clear, sunny day and the driving was a breeze. I was enjoying a variety of cassette tapes I'd brought along, in that radio reception in the north woods is nearly impossible. Although I was thoroughly relaxed and enjoying the drive, I was vaguely conscious of a strange, subtle feeling of being watched. There was virtually no one else on the road, and nothing out of the ordinary was evident within view of the truck windows. I dismissed the feeling as a latent result of the stress I'd been enduring at work: the long hours, the frustrating recurrent failures, and the boss constantly looking over my shoulder.

I arrived at Jim's camp in the early afternoon. It's a neat place right on the lake with a large open space for parking of vehicles and for boat and Jet Ski trailers in season. I settled in, grabbed a beer, and began to read. The environment was totally relaxing, and even though a few pages into the book the author's glaring affront to my intelligence had stirred up a level of aggravation, I soon dozed off.

It was becoming dusk when I awoke from my slumber and became aware of a disturbance outside of the cabin. I could see through the window that the previously mirror-quiet lake surface was now a series of whitecap waves splashing noisily against the shore. At the same time, I observed an unusual blue-white glow that was illuminating the foliage and lawn area surrounding the camp and that the light was much brighter than the now-ebbing sun. A chill came over me and my heart began to pound. This was all too familiar. I decided the best course was to lay low and stay inside and watch whatever was going on through the window.

It didn't take long to grasp what was going on. I was obviously in the company of another spacecraft, or even possibly the same one I had encountered in the squirrel incident almost a year earlier. It was hovering around twenty feet over the camp's parking area and nearly filled it, almost touching the trees that formed the lot's boundary. Although quiet itself, it had roiled up the lake as it arrived and was now churning up the grass, dust, and dirt in the parking area.

Soon tripod landing struts similar to those I had observed in my earlier encounter protruded from the bottom of the saucer and the craft settled onto the parking area no more than fifty feet from the cabin. The dust, dirt, and dislodged grass soon dissipated.

As in my previous encounter, I was at first overcome with fear and dread. At the same time, I found myself enveloped in a sense of wonderment and awe at the sight before me. (The beer I had consumed earlier might have been a factor too.) Reluctantly, I opened the door and momentarily contemplated actually stepping outside.

A minute or so after the ship had parked, a rectangular opening appeared in the side facing me, and a ramp extended from the opening to the parking lot surface. I anticipated seeing one or more aliens emerge from the ship. Nothing happened.

All Aboard!

I continued to wait—one, two, three minutes, and still no one exited from the craft. It was at this moment that I summoned the courage to step out onto the small front porch. I was immediately overcome with a very strong compulsion, an urgent need to leave the safety of the cabin and approach that spaceship. Summoning a strong will to do otherwise, I firmly resolved to not comply. The issue was soon resolved for me. Two Grays exited the vehicle, approached me one on each side, grasped my arms, and physically but gently escorted me off the porch, across the driveway, and up the ramp and into the saucer. In the process, I received a nasty bump on the head because I misjudged the height of the opening.

Once inside the craft we were met by a third and identical-looking Gray who positioned himself directly in front of me and stared intently into my eyes. The apprehension I had been feeling suddenly dissipated and I immediately relaxed. I began to look around. The sight that met my gaze was totally fascinating. I was awestruck. The interior was packed with all matter of interesting equipment and structures. I believe the Grays sensed my excitement in that they allowed me a few minutes to get my bearings and to look around.

It is important to note that much of the information I'm able to relate now, although prompted by observations made at the time, was only revealed to me in detail later. The means by which this occurred was the surprising consequence of an alien procedure, which I was about to experience.

The inside of the saucer was illuminated by a subdued white light that had no obvious source. The ship was roughly the same size as the one that confronted me in the squirrel incident, and it was beginning to dawn on me that this was indeed the same saucer and crew. I estimated that the inside diameter at the largest point on the circumference was around thirty feet. A useable interior space was defined by a region formed between a floor and the saucer-shaped configuration of the craft above it. I estimated this area to be around twenty feet in diameter allowing for a minimum height of six feet between the floor and the upper periphery of the spaceship. There was a lot of area remaining for machinery and equipment between the region formed by the saucer shape of the ship and the roughly rectangular functional center space.

The interior was essentially open; there were no partitions. A single ladder led to what I later determined was the cockpit or control room located in the protrusion at the top of the craft. The cylindrical bottom of the cockpit protruded around two feet into the ship's interior.

Much of the space was taken up by various assemblies and pieces of equipment, and there was barely ample room to move around for a person of my six-foot height and two-hundred-pound weight. I noticed a few items that appeared to be metallic storage cabinets extending from the floor to ceiling. The backside of the cabinets conformed to the complex shape of the craft's structural surface where they were attached. Some of the cabinets had obvious access doors on the front side, but others of similar construction had no observable openings. There were a number of floor-to-ceiling structures resembling hot water tanks mounted adjacent to one another along one side. Each had metallic tubes or pipes entering or exiting the top. These tanks were presumably for storage of liquids or gasses of some sort.

There was a small metallic surface attached to the walls that I surmised was probably a worktable. It was ingeniously designed to be stowed to conserve space, with front legs and an attached stool that folded out when in use. A centrally located larger shiny metallic table was attached at one end to a beam reaching from the floor to the ceiling. It was supported at the other end by two small cylindrical struts that folded outward to contact the floor and presumably locked into place when the table was deployed. The surface measured roughly three-feet wide by five feet in length. It was obviously configured to be stowed out of the way when latched in a vertical orientation onto the support beam. Some sort of apparatus (a panel and cables or hoses and other nondescript components) was suspended from the ceiling above the table. It occurred to me that this table could be the infamous surgical exploration table of many alien abduction accounts. I quickly strove to put that thought out of my mind. In that I had momentarily pondered the possibility, my alien hosts were probably aware of my concern.

In separate locations along the side of the craft were three similar arrangements of equipment consisting of metallic racks that housed sloped-front panels with what were probably controls and perhaps even indicator lights. These were mounted adjacent to and were obviously associated with some sort of complex-appearing machinery. The panels were probably a man-machine, or more appropriately an alien-machine, interface. Although similar in construction, the three facilities may have had different functions.

An obvious attention grabber was a huge structure that occupied an area from below the floor to the maximum height of the ship's hull at the unit's mounting point against the curved wall. The impressive edifice proved to be a heavily shielded nuclear reactor.

What I found particularly interesting was a grouping of four cylindrical columns adjacent to one another, approximately four feet in diameter, comprised of a clear glass-like material closed off at the top and bottom. The columns or cylinders extended from the floor to near the ceiling. Each column had a section defined by a dark thin outline that was most likely gasket material used to seal an access door where it connected to and closed against an opening in the column. Each door when opened would nearly bisect the diameter of the column. Each cylinder contained a small seat and had a cable or flexible pipe of some sort attached to the seat. My guess was the Grays entered these things for some purpose.

I was surprised to see a contraption that curiously resembled an exercise bicycle. *Is it possible that these guys actually work out?*

A rectangular metallic structure resembling a square box with rounded corners was located in the very center of the floor. It was an imposing item, measuring around four feet on

all sides with prominent ribs on all four of its vertical surfaces.
There was a coarse metallic mesh surrounding the item, obviously there to preclude alien body contact with the housing.
This I learned was protection from an extremely strong magnetic field surrounding a massive flywheel contained within the
unit. (It seems incredible that the aliens, with their otherwise
advanced technology, would employ something as seemingly
primitive as a flywheel.)   Flywheel/Storage

The flywheel, which spins at an incredible rate of speed
on virtually frictionless magnetic bearings, serves as a kinetic
energy storage medium. It is spun up by an electric motor over
a relatively long period of time, which limits the charging power
required. The motor becomes a generator when stored energy
is to be used, and instantaneous power that can be taken from
the system is immense. The enormous centrifugal force of the
flywheel also serves to stabilize the craft and to enhance the propulsion system's navigational agility. Strong pistons can almost
instantaneously change the spin axis angle, aiding in propelling
the craft in an alternate vector.

I learned that much of the remaining hardware associated
with the propulsion system was housed in the space devoted to
machinery between the functional center area and the periphery of the craft and beneath the floor with additional components located on the hull of the craft.

(Refer to figure 1 and also see figure 7: UFO profile.)

The air had a slight musty odor. I sensed a slight out-of-breath
feeling. This had to be due to the oxygen concentration in the
craft's atmosphere being lower than what I was used to in our
terrestrial atmosphere. The condition I was feeling is similar to

Alien Thinner Atmosphere ↓

what we earthlings might experience at altitudes ranging from five thousand to ten thousand feet.

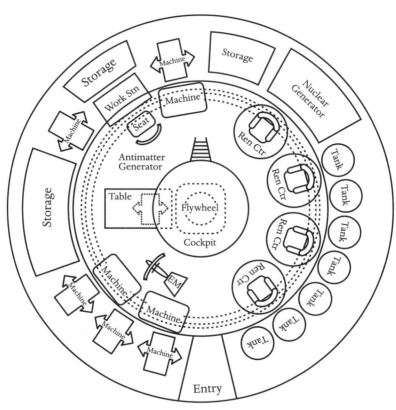

*Figure 1: Approximate location of significant items
of the saucer's interior from notes and drawings
made at the time. (EM = exercise machine)*

I was fascinated by the interior of this ship and would have liked to continue looking around. But the Grays had obviously decided it was time to get down to business. The third Gray was either the boss or the appointed spokesman, in that it was he (or maybe even she) that established eye contact and initiated the telepathic communication.

The conversation, if it could be called that, began with me being given the strong subliminal impression that I was important to the aliens and that I had been singled out for some sort of mission. This was accomplished in a very unique but effective way. The telepathy proceeded as follows: I began to see a vivid dreamlike image of a huge crowd of people with the likeness of a Gray in the right-side periphery. The image of the Gray remained stable as the scene began to pan toward one individual in the crowd that I eventually recognized as myself. As the focus drew closer to my image, the people surrounding me in the scene faded away until just my image and that of the alien remained. My image then brightened before fading out.

I then received the subliminal suggestion that the Grays wanted to establish a means of routine contact with me. The telepathic communication began with an image of me at home sitting in a living room chair, with a Gray entity again positioned at the periphery of the scene. The scene then changed to one of me at a workbench, again with the alien. The image changed yet again. This time I was at the dinner table, then in my truck, then lying in bed asleep (it dawned on me later that bedroom activities other than sleep could thus be monitored by the Grays), then playing with the dog. I was obviously imagining common occurrences in my life that the aliens were able to observe. The message was pretty clear. They wanted to monitor me in my day-to-day activities. I wasn't all that enthusiastic about being connected. How intrusive would it be? What would it involve? What benefit would I enjoy from this liaison?

For the first time in my contact with aliens, they actually seemed to respond. I was given a telepathic impetus to imagine a variety of unpleasant scenarios alternating with more pleasant alternatives. At first, I visualized a down and out homeless man, and shortly thereafter a scene of a recent college graduate wearing a mortar board with degree in hand, and this time with the familiar Gray in the view. I next envisioned my paycheck with five indecipherable figures in the "pay to the order of" section. The next image to materialize was a paycheck with six undecipherable figures, this time with the alien again in the scene. That mental representation then dissolved into an image of a forlorn individual sitting in a waiting room that I surmised was a doctor's office, with no alien in the scene. That impression morphed into one of an obviously happy and contented person sitting in a boat on a still lake on a bright sunny day, with an alien once again looking on. Okay, I got it. This arrangement could benefit me in diverse ways. So, assuming that I elected to go along with this (as if I had a choice), how would this come about? I was telepathically shown a human brain with a single line to a small shiny cylindrical device. I was then shown a Gray holding some sort of apparatus with a thin line connecting it to a similar small cylindrical device. I was then shown a combination of the images with dark lines interconnecting the two cylindrical devices.

The next few scenes nearly caused me to lose control of my sphincter despite the prescription-medicine-like tranquility I was enjoying. I was shown a telepathic image of the small cylindrical device being surgically inserted into a human being's nose. *No thanks, I don't think so!*

Apparently, there's no alien equivalent of "no thanks." I was escorted by two of the Grays to the centrally located metal table. I was overcome by the strong compulsion to lie down on it. This was decidedly a very bad omen, but I was in no position to resist. I complied. The table barely supported my girth, and because I'm considerably taller than the table's length, my feet and much of my legs hung off the end. It was very uncomfortable. One of the Grays approached the table and established eye contact. The dread and discomfort I was feeling soon began to fade, and I entered into an even deeper alien-induced state of blissful calm. I briefly pondered what was about to happen but was strangely apathetic.

Up, Up, and Away

The two aliens approached the table, one on each side. The one to my left withdrew a strap about three inches wide from a stowage point on the table. He handed the other end of the restraint, which looked like clear plastic, across my chest to the second Gray who secured it into a receptacle on his side. The belt automatically retracted, pulling taut over my chest. It was tight but wasn't uncomfortable. The two aliens then repeated the process using another strap positioned just above my knees. Okay, even in my alien drug-induced haze, this reinforced what I had instinctively surmised was a serious situation. It was all too reminiscent of accounts I'd read of alien medical experiments on defenseless abductees. I could envision all sorts of nasty invasive slicing and probing. I was shaking so violently the table rattled.

One of the Grays then went over to what I assumed was a row of storage cabinets and removed a small metallic box from one and brought it over to the table. The box seemed to have three or four small drawers in it. He placed it on the table near my head. It snapped into place on the metal table with such resounding authority that I assumed either the item or the table was magnetic.

The Gray then removed an instrument of some sort from a drawer in the box, grabbed my hand, extended a finger, and poked it with the sharp-pointed implement. It was mildly painful for a moment. After around a minute, the room appeared to twist and dissolve, and in a few seconds I passed out.

Some unknown period of time later, I began to come around. I was still strapped to the table and was consumed with the desire to be released and to get the hell out of there. Adding to my angst was an awareness of a pain that was growing in intensity just below my right eye socket. Two of the Grays were puttering around with something just inside the periphery of my vision. I hadn't seen the third one for a while. Anyway, they were all oblivious to my compulsion to put this catastrophe behind me.

Although I was unaware of it at the time, the procedure I'd just endured would have a profound effect on my life. One attribute was an uncanny awareness of details supporting observations I was about to make while aboard the ship. This ability often manifested during contemplation of a topic after the fact.

About the time I was wondering what had become of the third crewmember, he appeared from an area out of my line of sight and passed by the table. He approached the ladder that I had earlier concluded led to the spaceship's cockpit and mounted the ladder. When he reached the side of the cylindrical enclosure, a small hatchway opened and he climbed into the area, closing the entrance behind him.

Whatever analgesic medium the Grays had used was wearing off. Nearly fully conscious, I watched as the other two aliens approached the grouping of column structures I have called renewal centers. Each Gray advanced toward a different column, and when within a short distance from it, an entryway automatically opened. And, just as I thought, the thin dark outline in the column did indeed describe the boundary of an access port.

Each Gray entered his chosen cylinder and settled himself into its seat. I observed one of the guys tap a button on the seat's armrest and the entryway slowly closed.

I didn't notice at the time that there was no seat restraint evident. I was to discover that an innovative equivalent of a seat belt was indeed in use. A region of the alien's suit around his midriff is a highly compliant woven metal belt. Strong electromagnets in the rear and sides of the seat attract the Gray's belt, gently holding him in place. Inertia that would tend to dislodge the alien or move him from the center position of the seat is monitored, and the magnet flux holding him in place is automatically adjusted to compensate. Taps on two armrest buttons (one on each side) releases the restraint.

Nothing else happened for a few minutes. Still wondering what was going on here, I began to become aware of a slight vibration and then a pronounced feeling of being pressed into the table. It was then that one of the most profound events of my life took place.

What remained of my stupor immediately faded away. For some reason, I intuitively closed my eyes and was rewarded with an extremely clear dreamlike image of a plot of ground surrounded by trees, and a building perched next to a lake with a red truck parked nearby, my red truck. If this was telepathy, it beat the heck out of the foggy images the Grays had projected before. The scene was dynamic; items in view were receding rapidly as a broader scope of the terrain and the entire lake came into view illuminated by the last of the remaining daylight. I was obviously being treated to a vision of the area surrounding Jim's camp from the vantage point of speeding away from it. *Could this really be happening?* I was spellbound.

After a few minutes of watching landmarks and clouds diminish in size as the spacecraft pulled away, the curvature of the earth became evident against a dark and star-studded background. The mental image was breathtaking. The scene seemed to freeze, and the force that had pinned me to the table weakened and then was gone.

The fantastic image faded away, and I opened my eyes in time to observe one of the Grays as he emerged from his enclosure. He wasn't walking; he was floating! He slowly propelled himself over to the table I was strapped to and was soon joined by the second alien who approached in a manner reminiscent of a person leisurely swimming across a pool.

The Grays then did a most remarkable thing. They released the straps that had me immobilized and I immediately levitated off the table. I was weightless. Wherever we were, it was clearly out of the reach of Mother Earth's gravity.

What an extraordinary feeling. I had to grab onto the ship's structures to keep from floating or tumbling into them. It was obvious that weightlessness was something that took a lot of experience to master. I was allowed to experiment with it. I did somersaults, propelling myself from place to place with virtually no effort, and found a way to suspended myself with my feet against the ceiling. I was upside down without feeling that way. What an experience. The nagging pain below my eye was totally forgotten.

In the process of my weightless bumbling around, I crashed resoundingly into the base of the cockpit where it projected into the area below. The hatch immediately opened.

I was curious. There was no way I could fit my large frame into such a confined space. I found however that I could penetrate the space up to my waste with the rest of me dangling weightless below the hatchway.

The interior was large enough to accommodate two seats, a rectangular-shaped console between the seats, and a large instrument cluster in front of the seats. Behind the seats were three cabinets housing what I discovered was computer hardware and what I surmised to be a storage locker located above the computers. The area was awash with a subdued red glow.

The third Gray occupied one of the seats; the other was vacant. In retrospect, I presume the Gray was strapped into his seat magnetically. He was wearing a helmet that I concluded probably had a telepathic function as it surely wouldn't provide any sort of physical protection. There was no obvious wiring or interconnecting cable.

I pondered the fact that there were two seats and only one pilot. The intent was clearly to have two Grays running things. And it dawned on me at that moment that there were four of the renewal facilities downstairs and only three crewmembers. *Shouldn't there be a fourth member of this crew? Is the copilot among the missing? Did something untoward happen here?*

I was soon able to dismiss my concerns about the copilot and returned to my examination of the cockpit. The control panels were very cleverly integrated into the seat's armrest. When in the stowed position on the underside of the armrest, there was just the slightest hint of a seam where the two came together. The panels were attached at a single pivot point at the outer end of each armrest. In use, a seated Gray would swing each panel out so that it locked into place at a right angle to the armrest. When in position, the ends of the left and right panels almost met in the middle. This neat arrangement kept the panels out of the way for unencumbered access to the seat and put them in exactly the right position when deployed. The panels had a number of (alien) fingertip-sized squares and circles represented on the surface. Most were dark; a few were illuminated in yellow and blue as I recall. These were evidently system control inputs and status indicators.

A shaft protruded from the operator seat's left armrest that I took to be a joystick control handle. It was essentially a short post topped with a golf-ball-sized knob. A T-handle was mounted in the same relative position on the right armrest. The second seat had the same controls, but oddly they were reversed in position; the T-handle was on the left armrest.

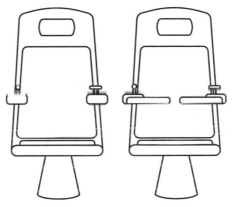

Figure 3: Cockpit seats line drawing: control panels stowed (L) and in use (R).

The instrument cluster was arranged to provide indicators and control devices convenient to each seat. There were five small viewports positioned just above the eye level of a seated alien, affording a forward-looking view in the ship's direction of travel.

What at first appeared to be two small video monitors were located on the instrument cluster in front of each operator. The screens provided two similar but different views of the terrain in front of and below the craft, presumably to assist in manually landing the saucer. I learned that in reality they were part of a passive system consisting of a periscope-like arrangement of mirrors and fiber optics.

The source of the image was two ports mounted on the hull in a downward-facing orientation in a location that would be impossible to access from the cockpit without the complicated periscope and fiber-optics link. The fiber optics conduit was comprised of thousands of tiny glass pipes bundled together to convey discrete packets of light (pixels, if you will). The fiber optics bundle was necessary to route the image around intruding components of the ship that interrupted a direct path between the viewports and the cockpit.

One would expect the technically astute aliens to use a sophisticated video system here in lieu of the viewports, but instead they chose a technique that, unlike electronics, would never suffer degraded performance or be prone to outright failure.

The cockpit's viewports were used primarily during times of terrestrial navigation. Although comprised of extremely rugged glass-like material, the external surface of the viewports was protected from particulate pummeling during deep space travel by remotely controlled external shutter devices. The viewports can be uncovered for short periods of observation during interstellar travel without incurring damage.

The console mounted between the two seats served as a storage cabinet and included a control panel on the side facing each seat. The panels contained devices exhibiting multicolored characters, icons, and graphics similar to those observed on the instrument cluster. The displays obviously represented significant ship status information. There were other unfamiliar items on the panels that were probably switches and controls.

The ship was slowly turning such that the scenes presented by the viewports panned across the sky. It was an awesome sight. The star field was intense against the total darkness of space. The moon was a bright sliver and to see the profile of Earth as it slipped by from this vantage point was an emotional, chilling experience.

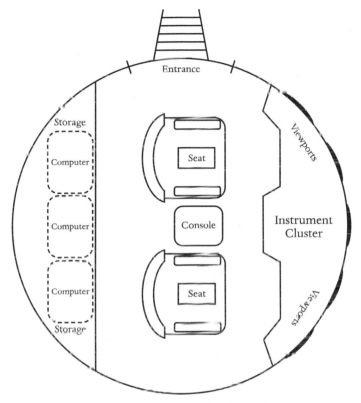

Figure 3: Approximate cockpit layout from notes and drawings made at the time.

I was momentarily perplexed by the realization that the windows periodically darkened, turning almost opaque. A closer look confirmed this was a protective measure as the sun passed into view at those times. The mechanism was a fast-acting chemical reaction to intense light produced in a sheet of material overlaying each viewport. The effect is similar to self-darkening sunglasses, is totally passive, and lends itself to uncomplicated replacement if ever needed using onboard spares.

Still engrossed in my exploration, I felt a tug on one of my legs. An alien had floated up to encourage me to move on. I withdrew from the opening in the cockpit, and the hatchway closed as I exited.

It was time to go. I was assisted by the Grays back to the table and was strapped down as before. The Grays retreated to their cubicles, and the slight vibration soon began again. The g-force again started to push me into the table. The imagery appeared as before, and I was transfixed watching the world materialize as we headed back. After what seemed like twenty or thirty minutes, Jim's campsite emerged illuminated by the spaceship's intense light source as we slowly decelerated. Seconds later, the ship shook slightly accompanied by a subdued thud and the vibration ceased. We had landed.

This thrilling adventure had obviously been undertaken for my benefit. *Why were these guys so accommodating? Were they just being nice, or was this payoff for some unknown debt?*

The Grays soon exited their columns and made way straight to my table to release the straps. I sat up on the table. I had long since regained full consciousness and was in full control of my faculties. Still, the aliens found it necessary to escort me, one on each arm, down the ramp and onto the camp's parking lot.

It was still dusk when we returned. In fact, it occurred to me that it was only a little darker than when we left. Considering that we must have been gone one or two hours, it should have been totally dark by now. Had I experienced some sort of reverse missing time phenomena? Then again, there was a nearly full moon that night. That had to be the answer.

Despite the fantastic experience I had been treated to, I was very relieved to be back. The breeze off the lake was cold, and I hurried into the relative warmth of the cabin.

The fireplace hadn't been turned on, but I didn't care. I was wiped out, my head hurt, and regardless of what the clock said, it was bedtime. I confiscated two extra blankets from the bedroom bureau, pulled them over me, and passed out. I may very well have entered my state of oblivion before the spaceship even departed.

Upon awakening the next morning, I was disturbed to find dried blood on the pillow. I must have had a nosebleed during the night and was embarrassed to have messed up Jim's pillowcase. I wadded it up and tossed it in my dirty clothes bag. Hopefully I'd be able to wash the stain out when I got home. Returning it would be awkward even if the stain did come out.

I had a vague recollection of the stunning events of Saturday evening, but was oddly unconcerned and turned my attention to making a sandwich for breakfast. The sandwich was dispatched in a minute or two and I hurriedly packed up the few items I had brought with me, including the book I had intended to devote more time to reading. It was just as well. At that point, regardless of the remarkable happenings the night before—at first bad and later gratifying—I'd had enough of aliens in print or for real.

As I poked around getting ready to leave, I became increasingly aware of discomfort in the area just below my right eye, but being prone to headaches and what I call eye-aches from time to time, it wasn't given much thought. I neglected to bring a razor and shaving cream with me, so the best I could do before reentering civilization was a change of clothes and to comb my hair. As I observed my combing effort in the bathroom mirror, dried blood on my right nostril reminded me of the nosebleed I'd experienced.

A little before nine o'clock I was in the truck happily on the way home, and surprisingly anxious to get back to work. As with my previous meeting with the Grays, it seemed prudent to say nothing. I'd be back home, back to work, back to normal. That's what I thought, anyway.

chapter four
EUREKA!

I arrived at home just before noon Sunday morning. I stopped by the house to announce my return and to clean up and shave. I harboring a guilty conscience, I planned to head off to work once I was presentable.

As always, I was met at the door by my furry buddy Rolph, our four-year-old mastiff. (He deafeningly declared his name at our first meeting years ago.) This greeting was far different than the normal excited tail wag. He appeared with his hackles up and barked incessantly. I knew I looked pretty rough and may not have smelled all that great, but still this was a very unusual and troubling response.

My wife came running. "What did you do to the dog?"

"Nothing," I replied. "What did *you* do to him? He's acting crazy."

Rolph eventually backed off and chose to go outside rather than tolerate my presence in the house. With the family convinced that I had done something grievous to the dog, it ironically occurred to me that I was the one in the doghouse. It seemed prudent to hasten my grooming and get the hell out of there.

I arrived at work about an hour later. The rest of the staff were there as expected. I was greeted with a nasty cold stare and the sarcastic greeting, "Feeling better?" from the boss. I headed to my office to grab a pen and my notebook and stopped by the coffee machine on the way to the lab.

The power supply project was still very much in trouble, more than I realized. We had won the contract for the unit by lowballing the bid—we needed the work. Our stock and trade were small electronic circuit boards. Designs operating at the very high power of this equipment were new to us. The thing was giving us fits. We were obviously on a steep learning curve. In my absence Saturday, things had gotten a lot worse. The boss had called an emergency staff meeting to advise that the customer was unhappy with our progress and was considering cancelling our contract and soliciting new proposal bids from other firms. A customer rep was scheduled to visit the plant in a few days to assess our progress. So far, we didn't have any progress to assess. Despite a number of engineering changes aimed at fixing the problem, the unit repeatedly exhibited a spectacular failure mode replete with a loud buzzing sound, copious smoke, and a myriad of red warning lights. We were on the cusp of having the project shut down. In that we lacked any other major program, it would mean pink slips for much of the staff.

What could very well be the last modification we'd be able to make was authorized the Saturday of my absence by Carl, the project engineer. Carl had a staff of two subordinate engineers, one being me. The mod had been installed and the unit had been operating flawlessly for a much longer time than on any previous life test run. People who stopped by the test area to check on the final hope for redemption were encouraged by the green lights on the test console, and a sense of cautious optimism prevailed.

Around two p.m. the optimism was dashed in a spectacular show of pyrotechnics. An earsplitting bang was followed by flame and smoke belching from ventilation louvers on the unit. The flames and heat were so intense that a schematic drawing lying nearby on the table burst into flame. A technician grabbed a fire extinguisher and thoroughly doused the prototype, rendering it a sticky hunk of scrap.

A staff meeting was hastily called by the boss within minutes of the failure. The company was in big trouble. We were going to miss an important contractual milestone and the customer was sure to cancel the contract. At that point we'd have to surrender the periodic progress payments made by the customer, and that could bankrupt our firm. Options and schemes for keeping the company alive would be considered over the next few days. For the time being everyone was dismissed for the remainder of the day. The project engineer and accounting personnel were told to report to work the next day. Others might as well stay at home. Human resources personnel would contact the staff as soon as the future outlook had solidified. That was it. There were tears and long faces as people exited the room.

I felt terrible. Although Carl had design responsibility for the project, I hadn't been able to suggest a remedy. In fact, I had taken time off on the last day that a solution might have been found.

I went directly from the meeting to my office to pack up family photos and other mementos. At that moment I had no idea if I'd ever be back. Some people hung around to discuss the dilemma. That was the *last* thing I wanted to do; I elected to go home.

Rolph was on his chain on the side lawn as I pulled into the driveway. As soon as I stepped out of the car, he growled, showing his teeth and barking incessantly. I doubted that a robber would be met with such disdain. There wasn't any reason to visit the vet; he was fine around everybody else. I must have gotten into something at Jim's cabin, maybe the hand soap or a cleaning agent that was for some reason irritating the dog. *Oh well, Rolph is the least of my problems at the moment.*

Bev was in the kitchen as I entered the house. "You're home early ... I wondered what was bothering the dog." I explained the plight at work and grabbed a beer from the fridge on my way to meditate in my lounge chair.

Bev, sensing my angst, attempted to keep the mood light during dinner. I was grateful for the diversion and hoped to find a TV program after supper to occupy my thoughts. I gave up around ten o'clock, kissed Bev goodnight, and went off to bed.

I awoke sometime during the night and realized that I'd been having really weird dreams. I recalled envisioning heavy duty physics concepts having to do with semiconductor theory and associated failure mechanisms. *This stuff bored the hell out of me in school; why would I be thinking about it now?*

I sat bolt upright in bed. I suddenly knew what was going on in that damn power supply, and more to the point, I knew how to fix it.

Validation

I was up early the next morning and grabbed a slice of toast and filled a travel mug with coffee on the way to the car for the drive to the plant.

The boss was already at his desk as I passed by his office. "What the hell are *you* doing here?"

I explained that I was sure I had a fix for the design flaw.

"Too late," he growled, "the prototype is toast."

I agreed but said that we had a second one in the lab that was missing a few components. I suggested that he call Dave, our very able technician, to come in to replace the missing parts. Meanwhile, I'd track down some parts we'd ordered and hadn't used for another job. We'd need twenty of them to hopefully cure the unit's woes; I hoped I could find that many.

Dave arrived about an hour later and soon had the missing parts replaced. I had redlined a schematic drawing showing the connection of the new parts I wanted added and Dave set about the difficult task of jamming them into the confined space within the unit.

A few hours later, Dave had the unit connected to the test bed and a party of onlookers including Dave and me, the boss,

Carl the project engineer, and two staff accountants had gathered to witness firing the unit up (a poor choice of words.)

The bottom line: The prototype came online and stayed online for weeks without a failure.

The customer wasn't apprised of the fix because we had no way of knowing at that point whether the thing would still be working when their rep visited the plant in three days. We were thrilled to have the emissary witness the unit churning out the amps, and we were granted a temporary reprieve on the moratorium. The project was firmly back on track two weeks later when a second visit confirmed that the unit had operated continuously for that period of time.

I was pretty proud of my accomplishment, more so than I had reason to be. I had no way of knowing then that I'd had help from a very unusual source. I was content and quite full of myself at being hailed as a hero. I was the toast of an office celebration. Our tightwad boss even sprung for a keg and salty snacks. My weekend transgression was forgiven, and I was awarded a citation with the promise of a raise.

The raise was nice while it lasted.

Sudoku

Sudoku is a number game in which the goal is to fill a nine-by-nine grid with numbers such that each row, column, and three-by-three section contain all of the digits one to nine without any duplication. From my point of view, this is an infinitely complicated game that makes my head hurt. My wife is an avid player.

I'd tried it a few times and found it to be way beyond my meager capability.

Four or five days after my weekend sojourn with the Grays, I was in my wife's chair watching the news on TV when I noticed a partially filled in Sudoku matrix on the side table. I was aware that my wife had been working on it for some time. I glanced at the page with wonderment. Why was she taking so long to finish this puzzle? I grabbed her pencil and was able to easily fill in the open spaces. *Man, that was no problem at all. Let's try another one.* I turned the page in the book to a fresh puzzle. Piece of cake. I had this one mastered in a matter of a few minutes too.

Okay, what's going on here? I had been recently noticing other unusual things too. Making deposits to our checking account is typically a struggle for me. I usually have to add up the bill amounts using a calculator a few times before I get two results that are the same, my check of accuracy necessitated by my tendency to be fumble fingered. On a few occasions recently, I swear I knew the total before striking a key on the calculator.

In the back of my mind, I knew what was going on. It was beginning to dawn on me that the eye ache and bloody nose I experienced after my last encounter with the Grays was from having one of the alien implants I'd read so much about stuck up my nose. The Grays indicated telepathically that they were going to do it at the time. I guess I'd been in some form of denial ever since, either self-imposed or perhaps alien inspired.

Although I was somewhat appreciative of my heightened mental acuity in some things, I was apprehensive about other aspects. For instance, I didn't like the gnawing feeling of being constantly watched. Most of the time I could ignore the feeling;

other times it was quite annoying. Additionally, some of the stuff I worked on was customer or company proprietary. I was unhappy with the possibility of this material being seen or possibly plagiarized by some other intelligence. I suspected that I'd be lucky to be offered janitorial work if the boss was aware of my situation. Also, trivial but troubling nonetheless was knowing that I was being watched while doing the silly or stupid things that often happen to me, like referring to the boss as an "AH" in an email that somehow ended up being widely circulated, or loudly exclaiming a forbidden word into the phone thinking my wife's lady friend had hung up. (Not that anything of this sort has actually happened of course.)

And there was the dog. In the weeks since I returned from my sojourn at Jim's camp, Rolph would have nothing to do with me. By now I'd showered and changed clothes enough times that whatever I initially thought I'd picked up from Jim's place that might have irritated the pup had to be long gone. *Was it just coincidence that the problem occurred right after my second visit with the Grays?* I doubted it. The implant had to be responsible.

I soon found that my newly heightened mental acuity was not universal and was at times selective. I still sucked at poker, still had trouble remembering people's names, couldn't do a crossword puzzle, lost money gambling at the casino, and couldn't pronounce the names of my prescription medicines. I could go on and on. And even more distressing was the fact that the effect was on and off. In one embarrassing episode I happened to mention my prowess at Sudoku at a party attended by my coworkers. Challenged to prove it, I confidently retrieved a page torn from my wife's book that I just happened to bring with me and bombed out totally. I drew a total blank. I was the laughingstock of the whole crew. Were my interstellar friends playing games? I blamed it on the wine, but I knew better.

I decided that I'd enjoy the benefits of this conduit to the extraterrestrials while at the same time maintaining a cautious attitude. Except for the problem with the dog that I now unequivocally blamed on the implant, nothing bad seemed to come from it; in fact, I was beginning to enjoy the element of discovery. And, besides, there wasn't anything I could do about it short of having it surgically removed anyway. Perhaps I would be in a position to glean information about the aliens that would amplify or clarify the material that often troubled me in material I was reading.

My curiosity was growing. About this time, I developed an even greater fascination with books describing alien encounters and abductions to the point of obsession. My reading appetite became ravenous. I even had a compulsion to reread some. It took prodding for me to lay down a book and attend to my responsibilities around home. I began to take notes to record my reaction to many of the details and descriptions in these publications. My attitude had recently changed from skepticism and disbelief to knowing for certain that some of the information was bogus. Not only did I have insight into the absurdity of some of the concepts and facts propounded in some of the material, I was often instinctively aware of more reasonable alternatives and explanations.

chapter five
TRIALS AND TRIBULATIONS

Over the years, I've been called to serve on juries a few times. On each occasion the lawyers representing the prosecution were quick to dismiss me when my vocation as an engineer was revealed. Apparently engineers tend to hold the prosecution to a higher standard of proof than the general public. So, when I received the latest summons in June of 1993, I was certain that I'd be released after a few hours at the courthouse. I hadn't bothered to tell anyone at work of my call to duty knowing I'd dedicate no more than a morning to the effort.

There were a number of prospective jurists assembled. We were told that the case involved a young man accused of robbing a liquor store. One by one, we were interviewed by lawyers representing both sides of the issue. My potential status as a jury member wasn't challenged by the defense lawyer. And I was shocked and dismayed to find that I was acceptable to the prosecution as well. I had made a point of apprising them of my occupation. The jury was comprised of me and six other men and five women.

The trial was to begin in a week. The boss wasn't very concerned about my absence from work in that the job I was on was fairly low priority. So, thinking to make the best of a new experience, I showed up on the trial date ready to do my civic duty.

The case was far from a slam dunk in favor of the prosecution. The accused had been stopped for erratic driving by the local police. Three unopened bottles of booze, all with the price information removed, were found in the vehicle. The guy roughly matched the description of the perpetrator given by the store proprietor. The crook had worn a mask so his attire, ethnicity, and general size were the only clues to his identity. Although no gun was found in the vehicle, the shop owner stated that the accused menacingly pointed a pistol at him that was concealed in the robber's coat pocket.

After two days of testimony, the trial was turned over to us to deliberate. The jury foreman was a no-nonsense retired food store manager who was quite obviously biased against the accused. We discussed points of the case for a few hours before it was decided to put the question of guilt or innocence up to a vote. The prosecution had skillfully made the best of a flimsy case. The accused was obviously less than a respectable model citizen and had been in and out of trouble for minor offences. Eleven of us were convinced of the guy's guilt. I was far from persuaded. The liquor store proprietor, whose inventory control was nonexistent, wasn't sure how many bottles were stolen and what variety of liquor was missing. He was "quite sure" the guy had a gun, which was amazing to me in that it was supposedly in the robber's pocket. He was "fairly certain" of his description of the robber's shabby attire. For me, this alone should have instilled sufficient doubt in the minds of the other jurors for an acquittal. But, encouraged by the overzealous foreman, they were ready to publish their guilty verdict and move on.

Over the next few hours, I attempted to influence the others of the tenuous quality of the case. The exchange became heated as I presented my arguments based on testimony. The foreman was close to outright rage. The judge was apprised of the deadlock and stormed into the jury room to strongly challenge us to come to a unanimous verdict or he would declare a mistrial that would represent a costly waste of time for all involved.

I stood my ground. There was no way I was going to assert the real reason for my adamant position. I didn't just doubt the validity of the evidence in the case, I knew for absolute certain that the accused was innocent. I had a strong mental image of the robber; it wasn't this guy. I couldn't overlook the recently flowering confidence in my perception that I knew came from a higher authority. There was no way I would chance sending this poor guy to jail feeling as I did. The contempt I knew the judge and jury felt toward me for the inevitable mistrial was difficult to shoulder. I hate being hated.

The trial and the subsequent decree of a mistrial made the news. I was asked at home and at work where I stood on the issue and in particular if I was the cause of the mistrial. I lied.

Raised eyebrows and blank stares told me that not everyone believed me.

Without naming the person, it was obvious in the press that the sole juror who screwed things up was scorned by the judge and the other members of the jury. The author of the article favored naming the individual. Fortunately, the court records were inaccessible to the public.

According to the paper, a new trial date was scheduled, and bail was set. The judge apparently took the defense lawyer's poor performance into consideration when setting the bail. It was low enough that the accused, who probably had very limited resources, was able to pay the fee and was released.

I fervently hoped that when this came to trial again the next jury would also see the folly of the weak and circumstantial evidence in the case. It would depend upon skillful representation in that nobody else would be privy to my unique insight.

I no doubt would have lost track of the case were it not for a strange irony. The second trial was held three months later and one of the people on the jury happened to be a woman who worked with Bev at the Five and Dime, or what we'd call a dollar store today. In their discussion of the woman's first jury experience, Bev recognized that the case was probably the follow-up to the one I was involved in. The accused's new defense lawyer was obviously much more adept this time around in that a not guilty verdict came down at the end of a very short trial.

As for the real perp, he apparently got away with having purloined a few bottles of booze.

Because of this affair, I found myself deeply troubled about the implications of my heightened perception. It's one thing to have one's capabilities enhanced in a technical area or to boost my prowess in a number game; it's quite another to be aware of things that could affect the day-to-day activities and well-being of other people. Having the wherewithal to intercede exposes a serious moral question as to whether there's an attendant obligation to do so.

While we're on the subject, I'll cite two more examples of my newfound prescience.

Potato Salad

Bev and I belong to a small local historical society. They maintain a diminutive museum with the traditional artifacts: an ox yoke, a spinning wheel, oil lamps, scrapbooks, chipped and cracked old crockery, etc. The group sponsors monthly meetings where members and occasionally nonmember authorities present talks on topics of local history.

The one much anticipated and well-attended summertime event is the society picnic at a nearby community park. It's a "bring your own dinnerware and a dish to pass" affair. To avoid duplication that has plagued the event in the past (three casseroles of baked beans on one occasion), food contribution is by assignment.

My wife drew the potato salad straw that year. Early the day of the event, I was sent to the local market to pick up a few pounds of their deli salad.

I was waiting my turn as the clerk behind the deli counter sliced meat and dished up salads for the customers ahead of me. My opportunity was about to come up when I was overcome with a strong compulsion to step out of line. *What the heck?* I was pondering this feeling for a moment while the guy behind the counter waitèd for me to order. The potato salad in the tray in the glass showcase looked fine. Why was I so reluctant?

Normally I would dismiss the feeling and forge ahead. But this time, in light of recent revelations, I was a lot more cautious. I apologized to the clerk and stepped away from the counter.

Now what? They're expecting potato salad. I had no choice but to head for the produce section to pick up potatoes, an onion, and a few stalks of celery. On the way, I passed by the canned food section, and there it was: German potato salad! *Why not?* I tossed a couple of large cans into the shopping cart and headed for home.

The reception upon my arrival was, to say the least, cold. I was soundly chastised for not having done what I was told. We could have passed off the deli potato salad as homemade if properly camouflaged on a bed of lettuce. What I so thoughtlessly brought home was obviously a lesser substitute that would mark us as lazy and cheap.

"Go back and get the deli salad."

"They're out of it," I protested. "I didn't think you'd want to make it from scratch," I said, lying through my teeth. I spent the rest of the day in Rolph's domain: the doghouse. (By the way, the German potato salad, a worthy complement to the hot dogs, hamburgers, and the one pan of beans, was totally cleaned out by the appreciative crowd.)

A few days later there was an article in the local paper revealing that a few local residents had recently experienced a food-borne illness, one case severe enough to land a lady in the hospital for a few days. The paper stated that the supermarket was "investigating the possibility of the source being a failure in the refrigeration equipment of the deli department."

I wanted to wave the article in a few faces but of course I couldn't; I'd be caught in my "they're out of it" lie. At the same time, it bothered my conscience knowing that I could have prevented the misery that befell the folks that got sick. But how? The store people would have either thought me crazy to suggest that their salad was tainted without sampling it, or worse that I was somehow complicit. Anyway, there was no reasonable way to explain how I knew better than to buy the salad. *And just how did I know? Just what clairvoyant source are these little gray guys tapped into and why am I the beneficiary?*

The Cat's Out

I'd gone out of the way to avoid any mention to family members of my association with aliens. I had no idea how I'd broach the subject without stirring up a wasp's nest of negative reactions that I wasn't equipped to handle. The family knew of my fascination with books on the subject. From time to time I'd tried citing details of specific cases of abduction that I'd read about as a way of introducing the subject. It fell on deaf ears; there wasn't the slightest interest in pursuing a dialogue with poor ol' dad on the topic. That avenue was a dead end.

My life had been profoundly affected by the encounter and the implant, and the ramifications of it were increasing in intensity and frequency. I knew there had been changes in my attitude and outlook as a result. I'd frankly been surprised that the family hadn't noticed. In fact, they had.

One fateful evening after the kids had gone to bed, Bev came into the room where I'd been watching a movie on TV and turned it off.

"We need to talk," she explained. She said that she'd noticed a change in me and that she knew that something was troubling me and that I was obviously keeping it to myself. She mentioned the disruption in my relationship with the dog and expressed her mounting concerns about my recent peculiar behavior and said that the kids had even begun to notice. She wondered if I was hiding a medical problem or if some situation at work or at home had triggered this difference in me. She wanted to know what she could do to help.

Okay, this was the moment I'd been dreading. There was no way to ease into the issue; it was about to explode.

"You'll recall that I've mentioned interesting cases of alien abduction that I'd read about." I went on to explain that I was hoping to acquaint the family with a few examples of extraterrestrial encounters as a preface to an important disclosure I had intended to make, but that she and the kids showed a perplexing lack of interest. Then the bombshell: "It has happened to me."

"What are you saying happened to you?" she asked incredulously.

"I've been abducted."

The revelation was met with a moment of stunned silence. "You're kidding, right?"

"No, I'm dead serious," I responded.

"You're asking me to believe that your recent weird behavior is because you were kidnapped by aliens?"

"Abducted … yes," was my lame reply. I briefly mentioned the details of my two encounters and the remarkable aftereffects.

Bev's reaction was pretty much as expected. "It's one thing to read and be as absorbed by that crap as you obviously are, and quite another to be living in the fantasy. If you really believe that this is more than strange dreams you've been having, you probably need psychiatric help."

She went on to remind me of the devastating impact this would have on the kids' relationship with their friends if word was to leak out, and of the probable dire outcome if people at both of our workplaces were to find out. As it was, she'd have to come up with a way to explain this to the kids that would avoid having them think of their father as a nutcase. "I'm begging you to please get yourself together and get help before this gets out of hand." She was emphatic that this needed to be resolved and that she wasn't about to entertain any further discussion about aliens and abduction. Then, in an abrupt change from her relatively calm demeanor up to that point, Bev looked me straight in the eye and firmly exclaimed, "Do you read me? *Please get this fixed!*"

Oh, I read Bev loud and clear, and vowed then and there to avoid bringing up the subject going forward. I know that she was genuinely worried about me, and I couldn't blame Bev for her reaction; it was perfectly plausible. I was aware of some of the traits I'd been exhibiting that the family had picked up on; I'd work to stifle them. I was dealing with a remarkable, if unbelievable, reality, and in my estimation I certainly didn't need psychiatric help.

The Elevator

I'd been diligently working at masking my alien-induced peculiarities with apparent success. Family life and relationships seemed to be reverting to their pre-abduction status with the notable exception of my ongoing problem with Rolph.

With the distressing situation at work long since resolved, and with the topic of aliens and abductions behind us, I decided that it was high time that my wife and I took advantage of a little downtime away from home. The seemingly endless days I spent at work during the crisis had made me irritable and unpleasant to be around the few hours I was home. Things that I should have been taking care of (mowing the lawn, shopping, paying bills) were left for Bev to do. It was time that I did something to make up for the torment she had to endure.

My wife often confers with her sister Kay who lives in a suburb around thirty miles from us. Kay was well aware of the ordeal we had been through and was a bit critical of me for devoting so much time and effort to the problem at the plant. She wasn't afraid to express her feelings on the subject at times when I answered her phone calls. She was also adamant in offering to stay at our house to watch the kids and animals so that Bev and I could get away for a few days. Her kids were older and could fend for themselves and our kids loved having their upbeat aunt come for a visit. I hadn't taken Kay up on the offer during the crisis, fearing retribution for taking the time off, but now that it was over, I was hoping that she'd broach the subject again. I wasn't about to ask though. My wife was more determined and approached her sister with a plea for help. Kay was willing and Bev announced that it was up to me to choose a date, a destination, and an itinerary.

Most people at the plant took vacation time toward the end of July. I decided that this was a good time for us to go too. I scheduled a week of vacation with the boss for the end of July.

We had visited New York City a few times in the past and found the attractions there, particularly off-Broadway shows and some really good restaurants, to be well worth the hassle and expense of a stay in the Big Apple. I thought it would be a neat idea to arrange the trip and then at the last minute spring it on my wife as a surprise. This time we'd take the train and leave the car at home. Driving in the city can be a white-knuckle experience and overnight parking costs almost as much as a hotel room. After a few sessions of lunchtime calls on the office phone, I had ordered train tickets and booked one of the few rooms left at a mid-level hotel just off Times Square. We'd stayed there before. The place was old, and the appearance of the lobby and its furnishings were reminiscent of the 1930s. The rooms were small but clean and the bathroom fixtures belonged in a museum, but the rate was very competitive. Our room was on the tenth floor with a stunning view of an adjacent building's rooftop. I prefer rooms on the lower floors, thinking in my overly cautious way that our chances of getting out in an emergency would be better.

I had the tickets and other documentation sent to my mailbox at the plant. Three days before the scheduled departure date, I gathered up the tickets and a couple of interesting playbills, stuck a red Christmas bow on the bundle, and presented it to my wife with the flourish that would normally attend a gift of diamonds. She stared at me with a look of concerned surprise. She had offered to provide the refreshments at the historical society meeting coming up in a few days. (This was the first meeting following the potato salad debacle and she wanted to make a good impression.) Besides that, she exclaimed, she didn't have anything to wear, and she wasn't about to go anywhere with her hair "looking like that"!

In retrospect, it might have been a good idea to have given my poor wife a little more advance notice. I can be packed and ready to go in less than ten minutes and I tend to forget that the ladies are a lot more meticulous.

It took some effort and a fair amount of schmoozing to straighten things out. I called the president of the historical society and explained the mess I'd made of things. She said that she'd be happy to provide the cookies and iced tea for the meeting. I presented Bev with my credit card and turned her loose at the mall. Setting up a hair appointment for the next day was more of a challenge. The hairdresser was booked solid for weeks in advance. A personal visit with a fist full of bills did the trick.

Bev was grudgingly willing to go along with my arrangements. Our teenaged kids would stay home, take care of the pets and, with their aunt as overseer, would adhere to the strict rule of no parties. (I guess I didn't know Kay very well. According to the neighbors there was a lot of activity around the pool until the wee hours and plenty of smoke from the charcoal grill those few days.)

Now all we had to do was pack.

Kay arrived in plenty of time to ferry us to the train station. The morning train was characteristically late, but we still arrived in New York with enough time to relax in our hotel room before venturing out for dinner. I took advantage of the time to canvass pamphlets listing stage shows we might take in over the next few days.

We had made a seven o'clock dinner reservation at a really good rib and barbecue restaurant we had discovered on a previous visit. Around six thirty we were in the elevator heading for the lobby to pick up a cab to take us to the rib joint. As the elevator doors closed, I was overcome with an urgent compulsion to leave the elevator. Obviously acting on impulse with no rationale whatsoever, I pushed the button that reopened the doors. I exited the elevator, expecting to be followed by my wife, who just stood there glaring at me. "What the hell are you doing?"

"I think we need the exercise. Let's use the stairs tonight," was my lame and not-well-thought-out response.

"You use the stairs; I'm taking the damn elevator." The other couple in the elevator were obviously amused. Bev had overlooked their presence, but having realized they were there, embarrassment got the better of her and she literally ran out of the elevator and stomped her way to the stairs, leaving me behind.

We caught a cab and had a quiet ride to the rib joint and a quiet time at dinner too. In fact, the only words Bev spoke the whole time were to the cab driver and to the waiter while ordering her meal and a double Manhattan. She was understandably upset and any explanation I could offer, especially the truth, would only make things worse.

The return cab ride was a pleasant experience for me. Seeing the sparkling colorful city lights and massive video displays on a dark evening is a rewarding experience. Bev must have felt the same way; she was speechless.

In around fifteen minutes we arrived at our hotel to see rescue vehicles and a fire truck parked outside. I inquired at the desk what was going on. "You'll have to use the stairs tonight. Both elevators are disabled. One got stuck between the fourth and fifth floors. The couple on the elevator were taken off just a few minutes ago. There was a short circuit in a power panel that exploded and won't be repaired until late in the morning."

We recognized the couple that emerged from the stairwell in the company of medics and a stretcher. The lady, who had to be carried off the elevator sobbing and screaming, had suffered a severe anxiety attack and the husband looked like he'd been through a tornado.

My wife's attitude softened... a little. "How did you know?" Before I could answer, she realized that she really didn't want a response to *that* question. In retrospect, I may actually have been aware of a slight burning odor in the elevator, although I know perfectly well that was not my reason for acting. *Thanks, guys,* I thought to myself.

We trudged up the ten flights of stairs, both moaning and cursing. We elected to stay in bed the next day until the desk clerk called to tell us that the elevators were functioning again.

The remainder of the trip was uneventful, nothing more was said about the elevator incident, and we fully enjoyed the rest of our vacation despite the shaky start.

chapter six
GRANDPA'S TRUNK

For weeks after my visit with the Grays and in quiet moments of contemplation of the consequences to my lifestyle—some good, some not so good—I would suddenly realize that I had been mulling over a disturbing mystery associated with the event. In my tour of the UFO's cockpit area, I recalled seeing a group of what appeared to be laminated glossy charts measuring roughly a foot by a foot and a half hanging on a hook on the side of the center console. They were obviously star charts, although the inscription along one edge was in symbols totally foreign to me. The thing is, they were somehow familiar. I had seen something very much like these charts before. But where, when, how?

I had been able to set aside the infrequent pondering of the mysterious charts in deference to thoughts pertaining to work, family, bills, and similar more pressing issues. That is, until one night when I awoke, being jarred fully awake, heart pounding with a flash of intuition. *Grandpa's trunk!*

My paternal grandparents lived in Maine. As a youngster during summer vacation, my parents and I, as their best and only success at producing offspring, would pack up the car with suitcases and our cocker spaniel pup, Grover (Grr-Rover), for a week or two stay with Grandpa and Grandma. I was young enough to have absolutely no appreciation of the elder family members' fascination with lobster, clams, and oysters. A hot dog or hamburger with fries and a chocolate shake was my preferred Maine meal. But the stay had its allure: my grandparents' totally cool attic. I would spend hours poking around in the dusty artifacts of a bygone area. There were old military uniforms, a box full of ancient-looking metal toy trucks and cars, an old wind-up phonograph with its heavy ten- and twelve-inch records, books and magazines, and aged wooden and plastic-cased radios that emitted strange sounds and foul-smelling wisps of smoke when plugged in and turned on. And then there was that trunk.

I had been told that the trunk was off limits and that it was locked anyway. For the longest time I heeded the admonition to steer clear until one day curiosity and temptation got the best of me and I decided to check it out. It was indeed locked, but it was also in really rough shape, having obviously been jostled around a lot over its many years of existence. The lock, secured by rusty screws, easily disengaged from the dried-out wood of the trunk with a little persuasion on my part, assisted by my trusty pocketknife.

Surprisingly, there wasn't a lot in the trunk, and none of it was particularly interesting to a nine- or ten-year-old kid. There were nondescript chunks of shiny metallic pieces, some with jagged and torn edges, some stuff that looked like tangled clear plastic spaghetti, and a stack of what appeared to be charts of some sort, marked with symbols in a foreign language. There were a number of books, two of which impressed me enough that I recall them today. One was a small, soft-covered pamphlet labeled simply "Survival." The cover had been torn from the other much larger and heavier book, which became the object of many hours of investigation. It had numerous black silhouettes and pictures and descriptions of aircraft ranging from biplanes to large multi-engine behemoths. Many were recogniz able US WW2 aircraft (B-17, B-29) but others were obviously foreign

One very interesting thing about the book as I think about it now was a pencil drawing on the blank last page It was no more than a curiosity to me as a kid, but I'll be damned if it wasn't an amateurish drawing of a UFO.

Of considerably less interest were a few letter-sized documents, brittle and yellowed with age, two or three black and white snapshots of men in uniform standing in front of a large pile of twisted debris, and an empty leather pistol holster. The thought of how neat a few of those charts would look posted on my bedroom wall briefly surfaced, but better angels prevailed. What a disappointment. I closed the trunk with everything back in place except for that airplane manual, and somehow managed to get the lock repositioned so that my transgression wasn't obvious. The book was carefully hidden in the rafters for perusal on future visits. For the time being, there were other interesting things in that attic requiring my attention.

My grandparents and that trunk are now long gone. Sadly, my parents have passed on as well. Of course, I now have a burning desire to know more about Grandpa and that trunk, and at this point there's no one left to ask. *Wait a minute!* I recalled that as a kid, my cousin Robert lived for a while in Maine not far from my grandparents. Maybe he could fill in some of the blanks.

We have exchanged Christmas cards over the years, and I had his address. Robert and I began corresponding and we talked occasionally on the phone. I didn't intend to fess up to my intrusion into the trunk or the circumstance of my present interest in its contents. The immediate family was convinced that I was crazy; there was no need to expand the audience. I cloaked my inquiry in terms of general interest in family lore. I learned a lot about various aunts, uncles, and cousins in the process.

When the topic I was most interested in pursuing came up, Robert admitted to a fascination with the attic too, and he remembered the trunk. Unlike me, he, being a fellow of more stalwart moral fiber, adhered to the warning to leave the trunk alone.

Robert was more aware of Grandpa's military career than I was. It was common knowledge in our family that Granddad served in the army in the late '40s and early '50s and that he was very reluctant to talk about it. Robert was certain that he had been a commissioned officer, at least a lieutenant, and that he was assigned to a unit involved in hush-hush investigations of some sort. Grandpa retired from the army after serving a few tours of duty and returned to civilian life to begin a career as a sheriff's deputy in the late '50s. Robert had a beat-up photograph of Grandpa in uniform, which he copied and sent to me. It was impossible to discern the timeframe or Grandpa's rank from the photo. Robert had no idea what became of our grandparents' household items when they passed away in the mid to late 1980s. Some very interesting stuff probably molders away, buried in a landfill somewhere.

And unfortunately that was pretty much all that my cousin could offer. What Granddad's involvement had been when the trunk items came into his possession, why he even had the material and where it came from was to remain a mystery.

Needless to say, I'm extremely sorry I hadn't been more diligent as a kid in investigating the contents of the trunk. In particular, the documents might have offered some insight into Grandpa's military career. And those other items should have evoked more interest. Obviously, with the connection I now firmly believe exists between the charts in that UFO cockpit and the ones I found in the trunk, I'm convinced that the stuff in the trunk was material collected from a UFO incident of some kind, and that Grandpa no doubt clandestinely purloined the stuff. Would I love to be able to confront him with this revelation. (So would certain factions of the government, I'm sure.)

I believe it's safe to conclude that Grandad was among a select few the army assigned to either investigate or clean up UFO crash sites in the '40s and '50s. *Could he also have had a rapport with aliens as I have?* It occurs to me that my connection with the aliens and Grandpa's presumed contact all those years ago may be a lot more than coincidence. And did this association, if it exists, skip a generation, or was my father also a beneficiary of extraterrestrial interest in our family? If he was, Dad never said, and I can certainly understand why.

chapter seven
CHRISTINA

Our post office closes at noon on Saturday. Over the years I'd developed a weekend routine. I'd plan to pick up the mail at around ten a.m., giving the postal workers plenty of time to have sorted the day's bills, store flyers, and solicitations for donations. Then I'd find my way to Eddie's Restaurant a few blocks away for coffee and a bagel or occasionally a cinnamon-sugar doughnut.

Eddie's was a typical small-town diner. The staff was friendly and knew most of their customers by name. Most customers, myself included, returned the compliment by addressing the staff by their first names. None of the fare at Eddie's would win them a culinary prize, but the meals were consistently good and the price was very reasonable.

On this particular fall day in 1993 there were a few tables empty. I prefer to be seated out of the way, intentionally avoiding the counter to limit my contact with the public to exchanges of "Hi, how are ya?" This was my time to enjoy quiet solitude and to reflect upon things without interruption.

I had received my order and was a few bites into my sesame seed bagel. A strange feeling had been building for a few minutes. I noticed in near panic that if I closed my eyes, I could vaguely discern a scene that looked very much like the interior of Eddie's but from a different vantage point than mine. I was seeing things, hallucinating! I'd had two sips of coffee. It couldn't be the caffeine. I suddenly lost interest in my mini breakfast. Hopefully if I got out of there, this would pass.

I started to get up when I felt a tap on my shoulder. A young lady was standing there. Even in the midst of my extreme distress, I observed that she was very attractive, around thirty years old with dark hair and a fair complexion. She was slight of build and casually dressed. "May I sit with you?"

I began to stammer a response that, had I gotten the chance to finish it, would have been in essence "No thanks. This is not a good time."

Before I could blurt out the first few words, she sat down in a chair on the opposite side of the table from me. "You have one, don't you?"

"What … have one what," I stammered.

"An implant," she responded.

I was floored, flabbergasted! How could she know about my implant? "How … what … why would you think that?" I sputtered.

"Crosstalk," she replied. She explained that where she was seated at a nearby table, she began to see a dreamlike image of the interior of the restaurant, and that it was obviously the scene from my particular vantage point. She had experienced a similar incident years ago, and it turned out to be due to crosstalk between implanted alien devices in two people who happened to be in close proximity to one another. Crosstalk was a more or less familiar term. I could recall as a kid hearing other conversations in the background when on the phone and being told that it was crosstalk from one phone line into another.

I was at once relieved to find that I hadn't gone off the edge and was intensely interested to hear the lady's story.

Her name was Christina; she lived in Colorado and was on her way to visit elderly relatives in the area. She had been driving her rental car long enough that morning to need a break and Eddie's looked like a good place to stop. She was married to an accountant, had one young daughter, and was taking a year or two sabbatical from her position as a public school teacher. Hubby couldn't leave the job, so she was on her own.

I was consumed with curiosity about her alien contact and was aware that this was a unique, once-in-a-lifetime chance to talk to someone who would fully comprehend the emotion associated with my own experience. Christina was on a tight timetable but agreed to meet at a municipal park a couple of miles away where there would be fewer eavesdroppers than at Eddie's.

Christina followed me to the park in her vehicle. It was a beautiful sunny day, and the leaves were well into their seasonal palette of spectacular color. We chose an isolated picnic table and began a most fascinating exchange.

She was a lifelong Colorado resident. Her family was outdoorsy, and she developed an enthusiasm at an early age for hiking the outstanding mountain trails in the area. On summer vacation from college, she and a few friends would often climb the familiar trails together. On one such occasion Christina tripped on an outcropping and badly sprained her ankle. She was unable to walk, so the friend who was with her that day agreed to trek the mile or so to the ranger station to get help. It was early afternoon on a comfortably warm day, and with luck Christina would be picked up in a couple of hours, none the worse for her wait.

She was picked up alright, but not by the ranger. The pain in her ankle was subsiding and Christina began to nod off as she sat in the sunshine waiting for assistance. She was startled awake by the sight of a huge metallic aircraft hovering over a clearing a few hundred yards away. Up to this point in her life, Christina didn't know a UFO from a clothespin, but there was no question in her mind what she was seeing. She was aghast at the spectacle.

The craft remained in position and slowly settled to the ground. As far away as it was, Christina felt intense warmth on her face that ceased the moment the ship landed. A ramp deployed and two beings departed the ship and approached Christina. The initial terror she was feeling subsided as the aliens stared at her intently. With some difficulty, the aliens were able to escort their limping charge into the UFO and onto what looked very much to her like a hospital surgical table.

Christina didn't remember anything beyond being led to the infamous table. She found herself sitting just off the trail where she had been when the UFO first appeared, groggy and with a pain below her right eye and dried blood on her nostril. The spacecraft was gone, leaving behind a circular scorched mark in the foliage.

The ranger, another guy, and her climbing buddy arrived shortly thereafter, and Christina was loaded on a stretcher and carried down the trail to the parking area. The comment was made that she obviously had smacked her nose in the fall that ripped up her ankle.

Christina thought better of talking to anyone, family or otherwise, about the incident on the mountain. Maybe it wasn't real. Maybe she had suffered a concussion in the fall. She was also hard-pressed to explain how she got such a deep tan on her face for the short time she'd been hiking that day. Now a bit curious though, she began to read up on aliens, UFOs, and the like.

It soon became apparent that this was not an imagined happenstance. Christina began to observe changes in her level of cognition. Some things that had been obscure to her she now perceived with a new clarity. She had chosen to become a high school history teacher and had interviewed for a few locally available positions and was turned down on them all. She was very highly rated academically, but the lack of verbal skills was her undoing at the interviews. Things changed radically at the very next meeting with a hiring ensemble following the mountain episode. She found herself expounding effortlessly on her background, her academic record, and her desire to benefit the community. She was surprised—no, shocked—that the interview went so well, and more to the point, that the principal and board offered a position on the spot. Christina was perfectly happy to have the benefits of the implant and was able to set aside the few annoyances that I, too, had noticed.

We talked a while about my background, my work, and my association with the aliens. We had become wrapped up in our mutual discoveries and discussion, and Christina was stunned to find that we'd been at it for well over two hours. She had to get back on the road.

I couldn't let her go without finding out more about this crosstalk thing. She said that she first became aware of the phenomenon on a plane trip returning from a friend's out-of-state wedding. She was sitting in the window seat next to a guy seated on the aisle. Christina was tired out from hours of partying and attempted to doze off.

As soon as she closed her eyes, she perceived a hazy image of a magazine article. It was familiar because she had been reading the airline magazine and happened across the same article earlier. She was startled by this occurrence. How had the image been burned into her retinas? She became alarmed and opened her eyes, hoping the image would fade in the ambient light. She looked over to the guy seated next to her. She needed to talk to anybody about this distressing manifestation, even this stranger. She turned toward the man and noticed that he was holding the airline publication, and it was opened to the article she was envisioning.

Christina paused for a moment. This was bizarre. The desire to talk to this guy was now intense, but what should she say? She suspected an alien connection because of other unusual occurrences in her life since her UFO happening. By now she was fairly certain that she had been the recipient of an implant she had read about in many abduction narratives. But mentioning that didn't seem very advisable.

She decided to engage the man with small talk at first. After a couple of minutes, it was clear that this was getting nowhere. Finally, she blurted out, "What do you think about UFOs?"

The man sat there in silence, an inquisitive look on his face. "Why do you ask?"

What the hell, she thought, *I'll never see this guy again.* She sat up in the seat and looked the guy squarely in the eye. "I was abducted by aliens."

The man noticeably blanched. "Why are you telling me this?" he asked.

"Because when I close my eyes, I see the magazine article you're reading. There has to be a connection."

The guy identified himself as Chuck and asked Christina her name. He, too, had been abducted a few years earlier. He was an airline captain on leave for a few days of R & R. He was on the way to meet his wife who was driving to a swank resort where they'd meet to celebrate their wedding anniversary away from kids, dogs, and distractions. He, too, was certain that he had been operated on to install an implant. He was also certain if the word reached airline officials of his alien involvement, he'd be sweeping the airport lounges for the rest of his career.

The two exchanged details of their cases. Chuck had been a naval flyer for eight years before leaving the service for a more lucrative career as an airline pilot. On one occasion while on a naval training mission, he had been confronted by a strange blue-white light that was able to dart ahead of and around his jet while flying at nearly Mach 1, which is airmen's jargon for the speed of sound, or around 760 miles per hour. He thought it better to not report the incident.

His meeting with the aliens happened while Chuck was on a deer hunting trip. His partner had given up for the day and headed back to the hunting camp a half mile away. Chuck had taken a shot at a deer that he believed he had wounded and wanted to find it. In the course of trekking through the woods in pursuit of the deer, the hunter became the hunted in much the same way Christina had met her cosmic acquaintances.

Chuck and Christina were puzzled by the visual effect she reported and decided to perform an experiment. Chuck suggested that Christina focus on some nearby object. He closed his eyes, and sure enough, a vague impression of a small bottle of booze materialized. Christina had been staring at a now-empty airline-sized vodka bottle in Chuck's seat pocket. Crosstalk.

They decided to see if they could determine the range of the crosstalk phenomenon. While Christina maintained her gaze on the vodka bottle, Chuck got up and headed toward the rear of the plane, stopping at each seat and momentarily closing his eyes. The passengers must have wondered what he was up to. Anyway, the effect dissipated completely in about twenty feet. I laughingly suggested to Christina that the aliens might want to issue a product recall to correct the crosstalk issue.

By now Christina was getting nervous about the time. She wouldn't arrive when she promised as it was, and she didn't wish to make the situation any worse. We exchanged mailing addresses and agreed to correspond.

We stayed in contact for a time but had pretty much covered all the ground in our initial meeting. Besides, I became concerned about my wife's possible erroneous perception of this relationship with another woman. The communication with Christina was cathartic, something I much needed and I was enormously thankful that we had met. But I decided to discontinue our correspondence and ultimately lost track of her. In retrospect that was unfortunate. I would really like to know if she also went through the grief I was to ultimately run into.

For the time being, life was good—really good. We were performing well on the power supply production at work; so well in fact that we were awarded follow-on contracts. We needed more people, and a hiring campaign was ongoing. The kids were doing well in school, and my wife had been promoted to manager of the dollar store where she'd worked for years. With the extra income, we ate out often, and rewarded ourselves with a few luxuries like his and hers snowmobiles. Rolph still avoided me, so the family thought I needed a pet and picked up a cat at the Humane Society. Emily turned out to be a lap kitty and she just plain loved me.

Amid all of this contentment, a dark cloud was about to rain on my parade.

chapter eight
CHILL IN THE AIR

As we do every year in early October, Bev and I took a few days off to tour the state's Adirondack region and immerse ourselves in the beautiful fall color. We stay at one of the Great Camps converted into a resort that dot the area and spend the days lounging around, reading, and partaking in the excellent cuisine. The return home always triggered the fall routine of putting lawn furniture into storage and readying ourselves for the transition from green to white.

Except for meeting Christina, for months there'd been very little to remind me of my alien experience. I was happy to put it out of my mind.

Stock and Trade

I had years earlier established a retirement account at work that was comprised of a variety of mutual funds. I had chosen the most conservative of the options available. The funds were doing okay, plodding along as expected for my cautious investment strategy, and I gave the periodically issued statements very little thought as I routinely filed them away.

It was sometime around Christmas of 1993 that I took particular notice of one of the statements. The stock market was performing well and the funds we owned were doing better than expected. *Great,* I thought as I stuffed the document into the file drawer. And then it hit me like a two-by-four. I might be missing a golden opportunity here (literally) considering my alien relationship. Okay, I'd found the benefits to be selective and a lot of things involving my perception hadn't changed at all, but this might be different. Why not take advantage of this potential windfall?

I began to scour the financial page of the paper. I was a total novice at this. I'd listened to guys talk about their investments at work and understood about half of the terms they were using. I needed to do some research.

After a few weeks of reading up on the basics and checking the market reports, the obvious choices for investment were pharmaceutical companies that at the time were hot. I chose an obscure drug producer and a medical holding company to test my prowess in faux investments on paper. Over the course of a couple of weeks, my portfolio had appreciated over 10 percent. I was on to something here. Warren Buffett and Bill Gates, eat your hearts out.

We had been driving a car that was beginning to spend more time at Harold's Hometown Auto Garage than in ours. We'd saved up a good chunk of change to buy a new-to-us replacement vehicle. And there the money was, sitting in that bank account earning a pitifully low interest rate.

The temptation was overwhelming. Should I invest the whole thing, or do a trial run with a couple thou? It was time to play with the big boys. I called a broker whose ads I'd seen in the paper and invested the whole shot; half in one company, and half in the other. I wouldn't tell the family about what might seem to some as a risky adventure. That could wait until I could justify it with the fabulous earnings I'd soon be able to flaunt. Talk about bringing home the bacon, I was anticipating the whole pig.

In the first few weeks, the stocks did very well, advancing in earnings an average of well over 15 percent. I decided to let it ride another week and then cash in my chips so to speak, bank the proceeds, and fervently vow to appreciatively kiss the ass of the first Gray I might ever chance to run into.

What happened was an ass kicking, not an ass kissing! The pharmaceutical company I had chosen to invest in was an upstart group that had recently brought a new antibiotic to trial. As it turned out, their antibiotic wasn't all that effective, and it actually killed a few laboratory animals. The word got out and the company tanked as a result. To make matters worse, the medical stock holding company I had chosen was unbeknownst to me invested heavily in the same discredited pharmaceutical firm. Their stock nearly tanked too.

I hastily sold my holdings and was able to recover the equivalent of a headlight and two tires worth of the cost of a new car. Apparently, the Grays don't follow the stock market. I had to come up with a rationale for my decidedly poor judgment in domestic court under my wife's jurisdiction, and of course without the merest mention of a connection with the aliens. It was an extreme embarrassment to have yielded to such greed. It was also another stark reminder that the benefits of the implant I'd come to take for granted were at best capricious. I probably spent more on the old wreck over the next two years than I would have for another car. We should have had a bigger accommodation for Rolph, because there were now two of us in it. The car, the much-needed house painting, and a new roof would have to wait.

Things went downhill from there.

The Accident

I should have taken more notice of the changes that were beginning to occur in me. Normally I would sleep soundly from the time I hit the sack until awakened by the alarm in the morning. A few times in late winter of '93, I found myself awake for no reason in the middle of the night, staring idly at the ceiling. These episodes could last for up to an hour before I was able to drift back to sleep.

What should have been of even greater concern was that I often found it necessary to ask people to repeat what they were saying. It wasn't so much a hearing problem; it was more a matter of foggy perception.

Doc Green had always been on my case about my excessive weight. I knew he'd be pleased at my next physical exam to find that I'd dropped ten pounds, although I had to confess I'd done it without really trying.

One change I began experiencing in the early spring wasn't so subtle. On a few occasions when driving home from work, I began to experience episodes of an overpowering cascade of multiple-layered thoughts that suddenly sprung to mind. It was so debilitating that I would seek a place to pull off the road until the incident would pass, usually in a minute or two. I found that the incidents occurred on days when I was particularly worn down by events at the plant, and always with the truck in motion; a sort of vertigo, I had surmised. In that nothing like this had ever happened before, I also concluded that it was probably related to the implant. This was obviously a dangerous situation, one that I had managed by quickly getting out of traffic, thus far without incident.

That changed on a Friday afternoon following a lengthy and tiring day of meetings and a plant tour with a potential deep-pocketed new customer. I had been on the road for twenty minutes and was idly contemplating a quiet moment with a beer or two at home before supper. Suddenly the now all-too-familiar jumble of thoughts materialized. The highway was lined with small businesses, all with convenient driveways. I hastily pulled into one, slamming on the brakes in an attempt to avoid the place's sign that was just off the edge of the drive. I flattened the sign.

The proprietor, a chiropractor, came tearing out of the building in a state of extreme agitation. I tried to calm him by profusely apologizing and vowing to write a generous check on the spot to cover his loss. He would have none of it. This was the third time he'd suffered property damage, and on the previous two occasions promise of payment was made but never happened. He insisted on involving the law in spite of my pleas to let me handle this without needing to report the mishap to my insurance company.

After what seemed like a very long time, a sheriff's patrol car appeared. The officer interviewed the doctor, and then approached my truck where I sat anxiously wanting to get this ordeal over with. The officer asked me to step out of the truck to conduct the interview. After taking down my vital statistics, and after hearing my version of the event (I'd fallen asleep at the wheel), he turned to leave, but then came back to where I was standing.

"I noticed the UFO books on the passenger's seat." Oh great, just what I needed, a discussion with an uninformed individual about UFOs when all I wanted to do was get home. I hoped to make quick work of this.

As it turned out, the sheriff was surprisingly well-informed. He had responded to a lights-in-the-sky report a few years back and was convinced that the witnesses were being truthful in their description of the event. He, too, had done some reading on the subject and was persuaded that stories of alien abductions were in many cases true.

Our conversation continued for a few minutes. And then came the unsettling and unavoidable question: Had I ever witnessed a UFO incident? I pondered how I might answer that one. Should I lie or fess up? I decided that a partial truth would do in that I'd never see this guy again anyway.

I related a *Reader's Digest* version of my first encounter with the Grays, failing to mention actually meeting the saucer's occupants, the finger poke, or the subsequent contact. As far as he was to know, I had been followed for a short distance in my truck by a low-flying aircraft with a bright light. I stated that I didn't know what it was. It probably was a military plane, although I supposed it could have been a UFO as well.

We exchanged a few more pleasantries and parted.

When I arrived home I greeted the family, told them I'd had a very rough day, and immediately headed for the fridge to grab a whole six-pack of beer. I retired to my lounge chair to consume the contents in lieu of supper.

In a few days, I heard from the insurance company. The cost of the doctor's replacement sign was under the deductible so I would have to pay anyway. That was fine with me; the premium wouldn't be affected and that was my major concern.

Something had to be done about these weird mental aberrations that caused this mess. I wondered if I should seek professional help. Which one should I see? A general practitioner or a shrink? I couldn't tell either of them what I thought was the cause; they'd think I was crazy. Maybe I *was* losing my mind. I didn't think my job was particularly stressful, but maybe it was. Perhaps I should ask for some time off. As much as I didn't want to, I knew I'd better consult with someone. I decided to make an appointment with the receptionist at our local family practice.

I had placed the call and was waiting for a nurse to schedule a visit with ol' Doc Green, who was a trusted physician and friend. Something occurred to me as I waited. These things always happened on days when I left work tired and run-down from the day's activities. What if I gulped a couple cups of our secretary's always-too-strong coffee just before leaving on those days? Could the caffeine jolt me into a conscious state that might prevent the disturbing occurrences? I decided on the spot to give it a try and hung up the phone.

It worked. The coffee did the trick. The troubling occurrences subsided. I was very pleased with myself. I had cured the symptoms through my own perceptive intervention. What I failed to grasp was that the underlying problem not only remained, it was growing.

The Visit

In that my wife and I both work and the kids are in school, there's usually no one at home during the day. I was surprised when our next-door neighbor Joyce, a stay-at-home housewife, came out to meet me one night as I exited the truck in the driveway. She reported that for a few days, a black Chevy van had been parked for hours directly across from our house. It typically left, parking further down the street around the time family members came home. She said that on at least two occasions it returned after dark, remaining for a few hours. She was surprised that we hadn't noticed.

I told Joyce that I wasn't too concerned but would keep a watchful eye on the situation. I decided not to mention this to the family until I had a better idea of what, if anything, was going on. I vowed to check for the van periodically throughout the evening hours.

Late the next evening, I peeked out the front window again as I had done a few times over the two days, just in time to see a dark-colored van pull away from the curb. I hurried outside, hoping to get a glimpse of the license plate. As dark as it was, there was no chance I'd be able to discern the characters on the plate. What surprised me was that there was enough light from the lamps on each side of the license plate holder to determine that there was no plate.

The next day was Saturday. The wife was working the weekend shift at the store, and both kids were off on their various weekend activities. I was alone with the cat and the dog. It was late April of 1994 and a heavy spring rain was forecast for the afternoon, so I thought I'd better tackle the hay field of a lawn before the deluge or I'd have to put mowing off yet another day. That prospect would be frowned upon by a certain faction of the family.

I was well into the task when I noticed a black Chevy van parked across the street. Okay, I needed to get to the bottom of this. I stopped the mower and was climbing off, intending to confront whoever was in that vehicle. The door of the van opened and a man in a dark suit exited the vehicle and walked up to the tractor.

Without identifying himself, he stated my name and asked if I was that person. I was very reluctant to answer and asked who wanted to know. He flashed a black leather badge with a large gold medallion and stated he was an emissary of a government agency. His mission was to advise me of the serious concerns his organization had regarding my recent behavior.

"What behavior?" I asked. He informed me that my disclosure of a supposed alien encounter had aroused the ire of principals in the agency. *What disclosure?* I thought to myself. Except for my meeting with fellow abductee Christina, I hadn't discussed my alien contact with anyone other than family, and the few times it came up they didn't want to talk about it. My son, Ted, in particular, and Bev and Ann to a lesser degree, genuinely thought I was nuts. They were embarrassed by the notion, so they certainly wouldn't have mentioned my alien friends to anyone who was in any way remotely connected with the government.

I was stunned. Who were these guys, and how did they find out? Christina was the only person I'd had any detailed discussion with, and it was unlikely that she had mentioned my alien involvement to anyone. Then it hit me: that damned cop, the sheriff that interviewed me after the signpost accident. He spilled the beans. He obviously didn't buy my "it could have been a UFO" remark; the pile of UFO-related books on the seat and the one in particular with guidelines for reporting an incident to a certain civilian UFO society must have tipped him off.

"Who do you represent?" I asked again. The response was something along the lines of who they were didn't matter. I needed to know that they were unhappy with any public discussion of supposed contact with UFOs and alien beings and strongly advised against any further involvement I might have with certain UFO investigative organizations. He went on to suggest the unfortunate ramifications among friends and colleagues at work if the word of my mental state that prompted delusions of aliens was to get out. "Take this as a strict warning to you and your family to keep your mouths shut." I had no doubt that he meant it.

He strode back to the van and drove away. I wanted to ask why the guy spent so much time watching our house. I found out after some research that these dark federal agencies routinely surveil a suspect's home to get an idea from the traffic coming and going how many people could be involved and how difficult containment might be.

There's one thing I can't dispute: men in black do exist. I certainly didn't want to tickle *that* tiger. Anyway, I had no intention of revealing any of this to anyone, at least not until a time that I felt my job and family were safe from the implied threat.

I told the ever-inquisitive Joyce that the van belonged to an insurance inspector. I lied, telling her that I had claimed a back injury in the accident, and they were trying to catch me in an activity that would prove I wasn't hurt.

Over time, the vertigo incidents would occasionally reoccur. They were much less intense and didn't interfere with my driving, but it was taking higher doses of coffee to keep them at bay. The caffeine was affecting my sleep in a vicious cycle situation that tended to aggravate the problem.

As bizarre and troubling as this was, it was nothing compared to what was coming.

To Dream ...

Around a month after the accident, another situation developed that would have a major impact on my life: very weird dreams. I would wake up in the middle of the night to recall recurrent variations on the same theme: scenes of places having bizarre foliage and unfamiliar animals, buildings of unusual architecture, and subdued, red-tinged sunlight producing shadows in two different directions. The dreams often involved an activity of some sort requiring an exhausting effort that could never be finished. Often, I would be in the company of antagonistic nonhuman entities for whom I was working. The appearance of these guys differed substantially from the Grays of my experience, and they were much more menacing. And, wherever this place was, it was uncomfortably dry and hot. I would wake up totally spent, soaked in perspiration, heart pounding.

At first these dreams occurred infrequently, maybe once a month and always at night. That changed over the course of a few months. By early summer, the nightmares had grown more frequent and more frightening. I would wake up from a daytime nap that I allowed myself on weekends, realizing that I had been having the same disturbing dreams. The lack of sleep was having an impact. My attitude changed. I became irritable, often snapping at family members and coworkers. I became unable to concentrate on a task. Things for which I was responsible at work—circuit designs, schedules, and deadlines—began to slip. Some days I didn't bother to go in to work. On days that I did show up, I was often un-showered, unshaven, uncombed, and unkempt. Numerous unpleasant closed-door meetings with the boss ensued, and my latest performance appraisal was a disaster. It was bad enough that I expected a pink slip at any time, although oddly, I didn't much care.

By this time, I had abandoned my reading, having totally lost interest in anything related to aliens. My hours at home were passed sitting in my lounge chair idly watching TV. My appetite suffered and I began to lose weight. It took sessions of wifely yelling to get me to even haphazardly mow the lawn. My truck ran out of gas on a couple of occasions. Our friends avoided us. Now even the cat was avoiding me. I was a mess.

I was encouraged, no, forced, to visit our family physician who strongly recommended psychiatric help. I was very reticent to take this avenue, mainly because I didn't want to face the probable diagnosis. I was pretty sure that I was heading for a one-way ticket to the funny farm. I told the doc to prescribe any medicine that he thought might help. I came home from the pharmacy with yet another prescription that I couldn't pronounce, and it had only a minimal effect.

Something had to be done. My job and marriage were in jeopardy. My mental health was in tatters, and my physical health was declining too. I began to actually fear for my life.

I was clearly a sick puppy. Bev had accompanied me on yet another visit with Doc Green three weeks after the previous one. I bemoaned the fact that the meds he'd prescribed didn't help. He said he knew the tablets would probably be only marginally effective but that I had insisted he write the script. He reminded us both that in his estimation my problem was mental rather than physical and that I should see a psychiatrist. Bev made an appointment and insisted over my vociferous objections that I go. I attended the first two sessions but stubbornly vowed that there'd be no third. Bev finally gave up trying to get me to go.

Bev and I are of different religious persuasions. I have never been particularly religious. I attended Sunday school for a few years as a kid, but as an adult hadn't attended church except for the occasional wedding or funeral. Bev regularly attends church. I hold the strong belief that there is a God, or at least an omnipotent and vast intelligence, and I am convinced that *everything* is according to some sort of master plan or algorithm. How could the marvel of the universe, of the earth, its life-forms, us, have just happened? How could a person with a lick of sense not believe in the existence of a divine authority?

As a youth, I was encouraged by my parents to say my prayers before bed. That was a very long time ago. The value of praying had been lost to me for many years … until now. My life was in tatters. I was desperate.

chapter nine
LET US PRAY

I began praying a few times a day, literally on my knees, fervently and seriously begging God to make this thing go away. I had plenty of time for prayer in that I had been fired from work the week before.

This was the last straw for my wife. My firing and newly found commitment to prayer just cemented the fact that hubby had irretrievably gone over the edge. My increasingly strange behavior coupled with my adamant refusal of psychiatric help was the tipping point for Bev. She knew that she had to remove our kids from the caustic environment at home.

She left, taking the kids, the dog, and the cat with her to a pet-friendly apartment in a village a few miles away. I wasn't surprised; in fact, I was sympathetic and vowed to do what I could to support them financially from our savings, even though she could probably have supported herself on her own income.

Because of her position at the dollar store, Bev was in frequent contact with inquisitive members of the community. She endured a lot of grief. The kids stayed in the same school district as before the move. This, of course, was a mixed blessing. Their close friends helped them cope with the trauma of a nutcase father, but they took a great deal of abuse from others. I deeply regret what this episode put my family through, far more than my own anguish and misery.

The regimen of praying three or four times a day went on for weeks, offset by hours of sitting stupefied in my chair with the TV blaring.

At some point I transitioned from concern about my condition, although I clearly wasn't prepared to do anything that might have helped, to just not caring. I even stopped praying.

Down and (Way) Out

What I'm about to relate occurred in late summer of '94 and much of it is from second- and thirdhand information. I have almost no recollection of the events.

Our town hired a local constable whose duties involved serving summonses, breaking up noisy parties, and making the occasional traffic stop. I didn't know him well but was of the impression that he was a decent sort, if not a bit overzealous in his position. I only vaguely recall meeting him professionally on a particularly unfortunate occasion.

I had returned in my truck from some unknown excursion that was at best ill-advised owing to my deteriorated mental state. I had parked the truck half on the lawn and half on the driveway, with the rear end blocking the sidewalk. To make matters worse, I had stumbled into the house leaving the engine running.

One of the neighbors who witnessed my arrival waited a while for me to return to the truck before deciding to act. He took it upon himself to turn off the truck and stepped up to the door to give me the keys. Getting no response after knocking and ringing the doorbell, my neighbor called the constable.

The constable showed up, lights flashing, as if he was dealing with a bank robbery. By this time a few neighbors had gathered as the constable banged repeatedly on the door. Finally, in frustration, he opened it to find me standing there, highly annoyed and shaking, menacingly waving my wife's BB gun.

Even with the unpleasant verbal exchange that ensued and the confiscation of the gun, the constable thankfully must have concluded that I wasn't high or drunk and that no laws had been broken. He chose to leave me to my misery and took it upon himself to move my truck. He tossed the keys on our hall chair and departed, lights still flashing.

As a concession to Bev who worked full-time, we had hired a housecleaning agency to come by every two weeks to dust and sweep up the wads of dog and cat hair. With Bev's departure, and with my now-total disregard for household cleanliness, the services of the local housecleaning company were sorely needed.

The two young ladies representing the cleaners showed up at the door as scheduled with their cleaning supplies and vacuum cleaners. After getting no response from attempts to get someone's attention, one of the girls stepped inside the door calling our names. I eventually staggered out of my chair to meet her, mumbling incoherently, sporting a two-week beard, needing a long-overdue haircut, and wearing only my boxer shorts and socks. We received a termination of service notification in the mail at Bev's next visit to the post office, as she had been doing twice a week.

Considering my newly acquired religious zeal, and although I'm not of the faith, my wife asked her pastor, Father Tom, to look in on me. She hoped that he could help me come to grips with whatever was responsible for my obsession.

Standing over six feet tall, in his forties, and weighing close to two-hundred pounds, Father Tom was a handsome and imposing figure. As an officer of the local volunteer fire department and as a member of the school board, the priest was universally admired by the community.

On the day Father Tom chose to call, I was remarkably wearing pants and a T-shirt and was sprawled out in a stupor in my lounge chair. Bev had indicated that it was futile to knock at the door or ring the bell. She told him to simply walk in and warned him of the abysmal conditions he was liable to find.

Father Tom approached my chair and touched my arm, jarring me into consciousness. I abruptly stood up, lost my balance, and grabbed for the side table, knocking it over and falling flat on my face on the floor.

Managing to get up on my knees, I began a tirade on what a bunch of greedy bastards the IRS was, and what business did this interloper have bothering me. I'd paid those crooks in Washington all I was going to pay. "Get the hell out!"

Father Tom attempted to convince me that he wasn't with the government to no avail. He then offered a short prayer—a *very* short prayer—and hastily took the advice I had so brusquely offered.

The priest called Bev to report on the hopeless situation he had encountered and to offer a glimmer of consolation. Father Tom would ask a member of his congregation and a fireman neighbor of mine to look in on me routinely and report to the priest any urgent situations he found that would require professional intervention.

I had met John on evening walks in the neighborhood, but didn't know him well. I didn't recognize him during his visits the few times I was even slightly conscious. John turned out to be the epitome of a good Samaritan. Not only did he check on me every few days, he made sure I had bottled water by my chair, brought along items like paper towels, and cleaned up my messes using his own mop and bucket. I owe John big time, and I was eventually in a position to let him know how indebted I felt. We ultimately became very good friends.

Glimmer of Hope

John's visits continued for over a month as winter approached. It was obvious that my condition was deteriorating. Father Tom kept Bev informed, and she was beginning to seriously consider having me committed to a psychiatric hospital. She had spoken to the psychiatrist I'd refused to visit for a recommendation and vowed to act in the next few days.

The nightmares persisted, and I was becoming weak from malnutrition although my wife saw to it that pizza and sub sandwiches were delivered to the house every few days. They all spoiled with only a few small nibbles taken out of them. I had become so emaciated that it was physically difficult and exhausting to get out of my chair. Bathroom stops that should have been attended to were sometimes missed with unpleasant consequences. Regrettably John, bless his heart, felt obliged to deal with the unfortunate aftermath.

Over time, I was beginning to become aware of John's presence on a few of his most recent visits and on one breakthrough occasion I actually uttered his name. With this slight indication of an improvement, Bev elected to hold off filing commitment papers for another week.

One day the same week, annoyed by a persistent ringing of the doorbell, I dragged myself out of my chair and stumbled to the door in a fit of agitation. The poor pizza delivery guy got a slurred and probably incoherent piece of my mind as he handed me a small boxed pizza my wife had ordered, expecting a tip he wasn't about to get. Heading for the overfilled trash bin with the unopened box, it dawned on me the darned thing actually smelled appetizing. A bite of a slice confirmed that it was somewhat palatable, and over the course of an hour, I managed to eat the whole slice.

That was a turning point. My appetite began to slowly return. The severity and frequency of the nightmares started to subside. Each day saw improvement and eventually I resumed praying; my intent gradually transitioning from pleas to grateful thanks that things were getting better.

Then it happened. Ten hours of uninterrupted sleep without the nightmare. I awoke the next morning rested and instinctively headed for the shower, a thing that hadn't happened in a very long time. Breakfast seemed like a good idea, but all I had was a piece of leftover sub sandwich, which contrary to recent protocol was in the refrigerator rather than the trash bin.

I shaved, put on clean clothes, and headed to the store to stock up on some groceries: eggs, bacon, milk, bread, and a six-pack of beer.

Back to Normal

Winter had descended upon the land. With the nightmares gone, and with food tasting good again, my stamina was returning, and the outside world was becoming of interest again. I began daily short-duration phone calls to my wife and kids and on a couple of occasions called people at work to see how it was going.

My interest in reading returned, and I picked up and began reading the book I had started months ago, the bookmark still in place. But something was different. The same sense of skepticism was there where a passage seemed outlandish, but the instinctual perception of alternative fact or a reasonable different interpretation was now missing.

Not only that, managing the checkbook became more difficult, and solving Sudoku was out of the question. I was back to the old me.

Thanks to someone or something, my prayers had indeed been answered. Did God or the aliens intervene? There were some troubling facts that needed to be faced vis-à-vis my alien friends' involvement, or lack of it, in this affair. Either they were aware of my torment and chose to ignore it, or the implant had crapped out and they were unaware of my agony. Considering the beneficial interventions early on, it seemed unlikely that they'd ignore the devastating distress I'd been experiencing. At that point it didn't matter. Whatever the cause of my malaise, it was apparently over, and I was literally given a new lease on life. I began to seriously rethink my prejudice against formal religion. I thought I might actually attend a Sunday service one day. And, best of all was the expectation that my connection with the aliens may have been severed. This was yet another misconception on my part.

chapter ten

CLOSE ENCOUNTER OF THE THIRD TIME

The phone calls with my wife had become more frequent, lasted longer, and were warm and friendly, and there were hints that the family might consider returning on a trial basis.

After numerous phone calls, and some whining and begging and frankly a fair amount of ass kissing, I had managed to convince my former boss to rehire me as a work-at-home consultant through a temporary hiring agency, also very much on a trial basis. I was given the challenge of redesigning a small subassembly circuit board that had a few now-obsolete parts, a situation destined to cause the manufacturing folks grief. A courier dropped off a pile of schematics, data sheets, and component manufacturers' catalogues. I happily immersed myself in the work. Although devoid of the eureka moment that attended the power supply design fix many months back, it was still a relatively simple task that I could easily handle. The project went well, and my changes were incorporated, well under the cost bogey and on time. I was promised a more significant task in the near future and a trial return to my old office. I couldn't wait.

About this time, I began harboring some very disturbing thoughts. Where I had dismissed the Grays' inaction during my illness as either ignorance or unconcern, I began to think that the little bastards may have actually initiated the affair as some sort of cruel experiment. The more I thought about it, the more convinced I became that the indications fit that scenario.

Meanwhile, the knowledge that I still had that thing stuck up my nose plagued me to no end. Being convinced that it had been the source of my problems, and even though things were returning to normal, I wanted it out of there. I made an appointment to visit a nose and throat clinic to investigate having it surgically removed.

When I called to make the appointment, I wasn't forthcoming with the receptionist about the reason for my visit. An appointment in nine days was made to look into an undefined discomfort above the right nostril. As far as I was concerned, the less said about what it was and where it came from, the better. I'd just have to plead ignorance (not a big stretch) if the surgeon was to ask. It was none of his business anyway. It never occurred to me that he might be inclined to *make* it his business. It did occur to the Grays.

Of course, because of my recent return to my former self, I considered the implant as dead or at least inactive. It didn't dawn on me that it might still be transmitting my thoughts, and from the aliens' point of view, having a third party interfering in their domain was a very bad idea.

The appointment was made on a Friday. I had elected to take Saturday off as there was no urgent activity going on at work. It would be a good chance to catch up on items around home needing attention. One thing that I had been putting off but was now suddenly on my mind, was a screech in one of the bearings on the lawnmower deck. The grease fitting for that bearing had been plugged for years, and lacking lubrication, it was finally about to succumb. It was May and the tortured bearing was unlikely to last through the mowing season.

The lawn equipment service shop where I'd taken chain saws, Weedwackers, and the like for many years was always able to remedy the problems in my aging equipment. Turnaround time was usually short, and the cost was reasonable. The place was a wreck though. It was pretty much a shack with a dirt floor and wholly inadequate lighting. A counter covered with assorted oily hardware junk, chain saw chains, spark plugs, pieces of note paper, and general clutter extended across one end of the place. Behind it was a large workbench also covered with stuff, and behind that, a number of storage shelves. The two cousins who owned the place could easily pass as brothers in appearance and mannerisms, and their constant chomping on cuds of smokeless tobacco lent a fascinating aura. Although they both did repair work, one cousin more often handled the counter, logging in the jobs and collecting payment while the other did most of the work. There didn't appear to be a computer. Work tags attached to items as they came in and bills torn from a pad were all handwritten. The place smelled of gasoline, oil, and perspiration. It was located on an out-of-the-way back road, but these guys were good enough to warrant the inconvenient drive.

So, after a half hour of effort the deck was off the lawn tractor, loaded in the bed of the truck, and on the way to a hopefully quick and inexpensive repair.

It was a gloomy, overcast day. I'd been driving for around forty minutes, taking it easy, listening to the radio and making the requisite turns without a care in the world. About thirty miles out, I realized I should have begun to see the recognizable farms and businesses in the area a few miles from the service shop. This was long before handheld GPS units were in common use and I didn't have a roadmap. Hell, I'd been there enough times, I didn't need a map. But there I was, hopelessly lost. How could I have made a wrong turn on such a familiar trip?

I knew for certain that the best approach was to turn around and hope to see something familiar that would put me back on the right course. That was easier said than done. The road here was a mini hog's back with a nasty drop off to a watery ditch on both sides. I didn't need to compound this by getting the truck stuck trying to turn around. A mile or so later, a grade level access road leading to a large open field came up. This was a perfect place to turn around.

I pulled the truck off the road and was instantly overcome with an all-too-memorable feeling of dread. Sure enough, up behind a row of trees on the far end of the field arose what looked like the same large alien spacecraft I had visited before. The saucer approached the truck, landing around a hundred feet in front of it. The truck's engine predictably sputtered and died. A ramp deployed immediately, and two Grays emerged and walked briskly to the driver's side of the truck. I was petrified with fear. There was no feeling of calm this time. I was terrified, and the aggressive pace of the Grays' egress from the saucer and brisk march to the truck spoke to a compelling urgency this time around. One of the two opened the truck door (I was surprised that he knew how) and forcibly grabbed my arm. The Grays' small wiry stature and lack of musculature would surely doom them to defeat in a physical altercation with a guy my size. But these guys obviously had attributes other than physical strength; they surely could immobilize an adversary telepathically. That pretty much trumped any thoughts of asserting my physical superiority. Resistance was out of the question. Besides, the impression that these two were pissed off came through loud and clear, and adding to their aggravation, whatever the cause, didn't seem like a good idea.

As before, I was led into the craft, and this time a lot less gently. Inside, we were met by a third Gray, who was probably the same individual who appeared to run the show in my previous encounter. These guys are expressionless, but even so it was evident that he was also agitated. He established eye contact, staring intently at me, and I instantly got the strong subliminal impression that I had violated a sacred trust or committed some other sin. The mental image of a pathway interrupted by a river or creek was transmitted to me. A bridge had been partially built over the water. A person, me I assumed, was the sole individual working on the bridge construction. The scene then changed; the person was gone leaving only the half-finished bridge in the scene. The image remained as pieces of the bridge then crumbled and fell into the water until the bridge was entirely gone. Next an image began to form in my mind of a person—me again—standing next to another person who was dressed in a white gown, obviously a doctor or surgeon. The scene then focused on the doctor's hand and he was holding…you guessed it…the damn implant. Okay, the message was clear. I had ruined some project or investigation the Grays had been conducting with me as a subject or participant. And they knew I intended to have their darned implant removed. They obviously didn't like the idea. How was I to know they were so sensitive about their implants?

The interior of the ship was pretty much as I remembered it until the realization occurred to me that the surgical table was missing. That was most reassuring. This had to be a different spacecraft and I would probably avoid being poked and probed this time.

The bubble soon burst. One of the Grays strolled over to what I realized was indeed the infamous table, which was stowed vertically against a support beam. He touched something on a panel and the table released from the beam and slowly assumed a horizontal orientation. As alarmed as I was about the potential use of that slab, I was impressed by its construction. It was comprised of two sections, one nested within the other. Its height when stowed was half of its fully deployed length. Once released from the stowed position and extended by the alien to its full length at the touch of another button, struts (legs) on the unsupported end automatically folded out, telescoped until contacting the floor, and locked into place. The Gray then grasped a shiny, rubbery, membrane that was spooled on a concealed roller mechanism and pulled it across the table's length, effectively covering and padding the joint where the two sections met. Even while shaken by the alarming prospect that awaited me, I was captivated by the efficient use of the space. The entire area beneath the table was devoted to machinery of some kind.

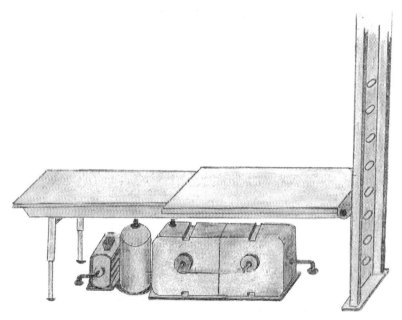

Figure 4: The table. (Machinery shown under the table is for illustration and is not an accurate depiction.)

I was escorted to the now-all-too-recognizable table as before and very reluctantly complied with the subliminal instruction to lie down on my back. I didn't want any part of what these guys were up to. Replacing my brief awe at the table design was sheer terror; I was literally shaking with fear. I was pretty sure we weren't going on another entertaining voyage into space.

What the Grays were planning was soon made abundantly clear. A telepathic image formed in my mind that roughly resembled the X-ray of a human head. Circled and highlighted was a small cylindrical object lodged just to the left of the head's right eye socket: the implant. Why were they showing me the implant? The first image dissolved and a second one formed. It was identical to the first, except this time the implant was gone. I didn't have time to digest what I'd been shown. The boss Gray grabbed my right hand and poked my finger with the all-too-familiar sharp object. I felt woozy and passed out.

I woke up somewhat nauseous, with a pronounced pain near my right eye and with blood stains on my shirt. The Grays were milling around but paid no attention to me. I lied there in increasing pain, slowly regaining my faculties. Eventually, the two subordinate Grays approached the table and assisted me in sitting up. Obviously aware of my shaky condition, they retreated, leaving me sitting there anxious and uncomfortable. After what seemed like an interminably long time, the two appeared and assisted me in standing. Still a little wobbly, I was escorted back to my truck.

I waited in the truck for the saucer to depart and for my head to clear. The truck wouldn't start until they left anyway. In a few minutes the ramp was withdrawn, and the saucer levitated a few feet off the ground as the landing pods were retracted. The craft then shot straight upward, tilted slightly, and was gone in an instant. Still quite groggy when I entered the truck, I had forgotten the admonition given at the previous encounter to close the truck doors and windows during the craft's departure. This was just another painful mistake in judgment on my part.

I sported a deep suntan on the left side of my face for weeks. In retrospect, I surmise that the radiation that cooks the foliage so often reported at a UFO landing site probably caused the burn. A likely candidate would be very short wavelength ultraviolet light (UV) that would normally be blocked by window glass. Anyway, the craft was gone, and I hoped, and yes prayed, that it stayed that way.

Eventually I felt confident enough in my driving ability to turn around and head back in the other direction. A few miles down the road, a driveway materialized with a house, barn, and outbuildings. I pulled in and knocked on the door. A young woman answered who was visibly shocked at my appearance. My intent was to get directions to a route I was familiar with so I could find my way home. The young lady was sure that I was seeking medical help. She asked how and where the accident happened and if there were any other injured people. It took a lot of persuasion to convince her that I was alone and okay and just wanted driving instructions. With directions written on a piece of lined notebook paper, I headed for home.

Sometime later I arrived home with the mower deck still in the back of the truck. That could wait for another day. The next time I'd bring a map. A look in the mirror confirmed the reason for the concern the young lady had expressed. With one side of my face sunburned, dried blood caked on my right nostril, my shirt covered in blood splatters, and my hair totally disheveled, I was one sad sack sight to behold. At least there was no one home expecting a plausible explanation for what was a totally implausible situation. I found it hard to believe myself. In the weeks following the last unfortunate incident, I continued communication with my wife and eventually convinced her that I was reasonably sane. She and the kids and good ol' Rolph and Emily returned. After a brief period to get reacquainted, the dog and I resumed our former pre-alien relationship. Emily resumed lap cat duties immediately. The subject of my out-of-this-world experience has only come up a few times. I was content in keeping it to myself. I was put through hell; I lost my mind and my health for a time and really believe I was on the cusp of my own demise. The affair drove my family away for months, and I came perilously close to permanently losing the job I love and my sole source of income. It was all in the past though, and I was able to put it behind me. What the Grays found of interest in me, why they put me through that devastating ordeal, and the virtue of tapping into my psyche was never revealed.

With the passage of time, our family life took a predictable course. The kids graduated from high school and our daughter attended college and went on to become a grade school teacher. Our son took up auto mechanics and established a successful business out of state. Bev and I have both retired. Ours is a very comfortable lifestyle. She's involved in various civic organizations, and I get dragged along to assist where I can. With the typical domestic chores and the volunteer work, we're easily able to stave off boredom.

As time passed, I still maintained my interest in reading accounts of alien contact and abduction. In later years, the Internet provided a rich source of material in addition to the books I found informative. Interviews with enlightened sources and videos of speakers at UFO conferences offered a unique perspective on the personality of the presenters that can't be inferred from the printed page. Many could be easily dismissed as unreliable; others offered fascinating and compelling narratives. I closely followed the writers and internet presenters whom I found to be credible. It was exciting and gratifying to witness reputable individuals, particularly former military officers and other high-ranking professionals, expound on their alien connection. So much so that on occasion I arranged to be in the audience at a few UFO conventions. I even reached out to individuals that had particularly compelling accounts. Still being concerned, even in retirement, about the repercussions of coming out, I was happy to take advantage of the anonymity of the internet in these exchanges.

Surprisingly, in all of those years of following the output of others, it never occurred to me that I might have something valuable to offer. The copious notes taken during my alien happening had been gathered and boxed up with a few of the books I found particularly interesting. Long forgotten, the box sat on a cellar shelf collecting dust. One day while poking around in an effort to locate a box of heirloom china that Bev wanted to display, I happened upon the alien stuff. A vague thought materialized. I had always considered the details of my encounters far more informative and interesting than most of the things I'd read. Thanks to that damnable implant, I had been afforded a unique insight into the Grays. Perhaps some real benefit could come from the plethora of knowledge I'd acquired through that channel. If my notes were as concise and detailed as I recalled, maybe I should consider putting together an account of my extra-terrestrial history. The box was dusted off, and thus began months of becoming reacquainted with and organizing the documentation, and untold hours banging away at the computer keyboard. The result is what you're reading.

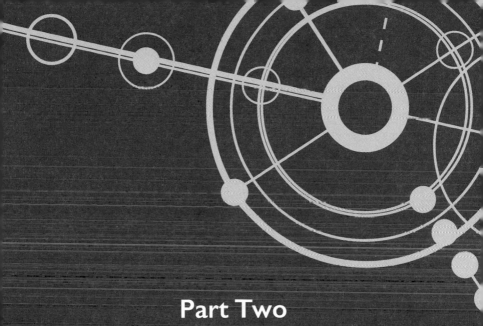

Part Two
OBSERVATIONS

chapter eleven
DETAILS, DETAILS

To some degree in previous chapters and to a substantial extent in the next few, a great deal of information is revealed about the Grays and their spaceship. The reader would be justified in asking what makes me an authority. The simple answer is the Grays themselves; the reason is more complicated.

From the moment I stepped out of my truck in the first encounter while relocating that squirrel, I became part of an elaborate extraterrestrial experiment. Something in my genetic makeup must have been revealed in the hair and tissue sample taken that day, which committed me to their project. My life-long interest in space and UFOs, and perhaps the family connection (Grandpa) may have been a factor too.

The device the Grays had surgically implanted in the second meeting aboard their spaceship allowed them to monitor my thought patterns and instill concepts and suggestions of their choosing.

At first the aliens' intervention was beneficial, beginning with the extraordinary tour of their ship and the thrilling experience of weightlessness.

My solution to the problem at work, my mastery of Sudoku, and the incident at the deli must have been aimed at assessing my reaction to the positive implications of the implant. So, too, was my extraordinary access to a plethora of information. Details about the aliens' physiology and technical aspects of their spaceship, some of which would normally not have concerned or interested me, were accessible to instant recall in the same way as our knowledge of the alphabet or the names and order of the months. In this case, however, the learning step was bypassed. When a topic came up, the information was just there. The aliens must have been interested in what I'd do with this gift. I wonder if they envisioned this book; they surely could have prevented it from happening.

There's another aspect of this too. The aliens put me through hell—on purpose—probably to gauge my reaction to extreme adversity. It was cruel and lacked the slightest modicum of compassion. I have resigned myself to believing that they were emotionally predisposed to a lack of sensitivity rather than having exhibited either disregard or outright malice. I ultimately recovered from the trauma but have wondered how close I came to a tragic outcome. In any event, my prescience into alien affairs may have been rendered as a form of compensation for my ordeal.

So, the information in part two comes from extensive reading, observations made aboard alien spacecraft, and points pondered after the fact, all buttressed by the insight gained via the implant.

Meet the Grays

Unquestionably, the most common alien life-form described and depicted in books, publications, on TV, in the movies, on greeting cards—virtually everywhere, is the Grays. They are the aliens most often sketched by people claiming an encounter. They are the aliens said to have crashed at Roswell, New Mexico, in 1947, one having purportedly survived his injuries long enough to have been the subject of scientific research. While other alien life-forms are reported in the media (tall scaly reptilians, giant humanoids, blond-haired Nordic types, and menacing mantis insectoids to name a few), it is the Grays that are the cosmic explorers we earthlings seem to encounter most often.

The Grays have been described in detail in print, and the information gathered from various sources seems to be well correlated. However, some depictions of the Grays have their heads appearing to be egg-shaped. I was able to observe these guys up close and personal on my three visits with them. Perhaps there's more than one race of gray-tinged aliens because the ones I met were definitely not eggheads. The drawing below illustrates two of the three Grays I named "Bud," "Burt," and "Boss," although I couldn't really tell them apart.

In referring to the notes consisting of information gathered with the aid and assistance of the aliens during my encounters, and in studious reflection after the fact, I'm able to offer the description that follows of these incredibly interesting beings.

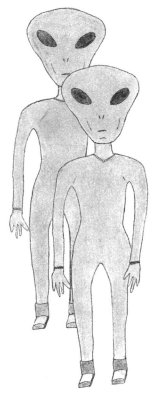

Figure 5: The Grays.

Vital Statistics

The Grays are not robotic. They are living beings genetically engineered expressly as cosmic explorers. They have no other expectation in life and appear to have entered into this form of servitude willingly. Perhaps acceptance of their fate is inbred. The Grays I encountered all appeared to be identical and may very well have been clones. They can be considered bionic to the extent that they have had surgery to add a combined feeding tube and body waste removal port. Their source DNA probably came from their home planet masters who are probably superior emotionally and intellectually. Just how similar the Grays are to them was not revealed to me.

They are physiologically compatible with the temperature range and atmospheric content of worlds such as ours. Their lifetime is very long compared to ours, a necessary attribute for a species that traverses great distances and takes a long, long time doing it.

As mentioned earlier, Grays are diminutive in size, having been called childlike in stature. Their complexion ranges from dark gray to a medium shade. They lack defined musculature; their legs are short, having joint placement that differs considerably from humans. They have a small chest, proportionally long arms, and hands with a thumb and three fingers.

Their heads are large in proportion to their bodies. The most prominent facial feature is their large, somewhat slanted, dark and opaque eyes. They lack an external nose, although two small orifices exist where nostrils would normally be found. They have no external ears, although small indentations can be seen where ears would be expected. They may be able to hear a limited range of frequencies. They have a tiny mouth, probably not functional for eating or speech, and extremely thin lips.

Grays don't reproduce and have no sex organs. Although referred to as "he" here, they are neither male nor female. They have no urinary orifice (penis) or anus.

They have no body hair. The indices of age we humans experience (graying or diminished hair and wrinkles) wouldn't manifest in the Grays. It might be impossible to gauge the extent of their maturity by sight.

They breathe an atmosphere of nitrogen and oxygen but require substantially less oxygen than humans due primarily to their low body mass and avoidance of physical exertion. Earth's oxygen percentage (around 20 percent) could be detrimental to Grays over very long exposure, and they purposely limit time spent in our atmosphere.

Grays have a circulatory system. Their bone marrow produces red blood cells containing hemoglobin. The red cells are actually a light pink in color, thus contributing to their gray skin tone. They probably can feel pain and would bleed if their flesh was cut. In that the aliens are almost certainly clones, they'd all have the same blood type.

The Grays are not prone to viral or bacterial disease due in part to their closed environment but also their very effective health monitoring and remediation facilities. What is remarkable: they subject themselves to our pathogens by exiting their craft without a helmet or respirator, and presumably take on water from terrestrial sources although it's no doubt sterilized for consumption. Most surprising, their work here involves contact with germy humans, and they perform surgical procedures on us (at least to insert implants and possibly other oft-reported probing) that could release our blood into their environment. How they avoid contracting our diseases is a mystery. If they've developed the medicinal agents or antibodies to combat terrestrial bugs, it would be a monumental windfall for us to be allowed to avail ourselves of them.

Their large eyes may be more sensitive than ours, may accommodate a greater dynamic range, and could also provide higher-definition and greater peripheral vision. Just what advantage these attributes would be to their mission wasn't apparent to me; they may relate more to conditions peculiar to their home planet. Their vision, like ours, is binocular. They see color as was amply demonstrated by the multicolored icons on their cockpit status panels. They probably perceive light that is invisible to us at one or both extremes of the spectrum. As pointed out earlier, their eyes are undoubtedly involved in their telepathic capabilities.

I was initially convinced that the Grays were ambidextrous based primarily on the reversal of position of the joystick and T-handle controls on the two cockpit seat armrests and the assumption that an airline-typical pilot/copilot configuration in the wheelhouse was the norm. If the functions were redundant, the reversal would suggest that left/right orientation is meaningless to the aliens. Oddly, though, as I noted during my joyride experience, there was only one Gray in the cockpit, so a copilot isn't always needed. The controls might conceivably be configured for different functions so that the two aliens could share piloting responsibilities. A mission in which the spaceship and the drone (discussed later) are both in flight is an example. The reversal makes sense in this scenario. It would be obvious that the joystick and T-handle functions were unique to a peculiar seat. This would reduce the possibility of confusing the roles of the devices. The ambidextrous theory is supported in this situation too. One far less plausible explanation for the enigma is an accommodation of alien left- or right-handedness wherein the Gray chooses a seat according to his predilection. This of course would be absurdly wasteful of resources. Another just slightly less implausible possibility is that the controls could be swapped from one side to the other on a whim for operator convenience. Anyway, the controls may only be a backup to telepathic input from the headgear my pilot was wearing, so the placement rationale remains a mystery.

Nutrition

Grays virtually never eat food. Nourishment is provided and waste removal is accomplished via interfaces into shipboard systems through a surgically added interface port located on their abdomen.

Nourishment is delivered in the form of a suspension of water and a yeast-like substance. The nutrient is self-perpetuating, much as a yogurt culture is maintained by humans by routinely committing a small portion of it to renew the culture. Dedicated equipment produces the product, which is then stored in a containment vessel under precise environmental control. The agent supporting the growth of the culture is made from—this may seem gross—sterilized and processed components extracted from the aliens' excrement. The raw culture is stored as a dry powder and is there as a backup for emergency use in the unlikely case that something goes awry with the active culture. With proper execution of the process, the backup would never be needed.

Special chambers that I call "renewal centers" serve as a combined health monitoring, maintenance facility, and crew quarters or, more accurately, a crew seating area. The facilities consist of multiple (at least one for each crewmember) floor-to-ceiling cylindrical enclosures of clear glass-like material with an entry door that seals the structure. Each cylinder is outfitted with a seat with control buttons on the armrests, an umbilical cable that provides the nutritional product and carries away waste, and a unique display device.

The display facility in the renewal center is clever. Characters (which were foreign to me) are either projected onto the clear material comprising the column or produced in a medium similar to the liquid crystal display on our digital watches. The figures are shown in bright green directly in the line of sight of the occupant. I could see no wiring or obvious sign of pixels when the device was in use or was inactive. I should note that I was observing the display from outside of the center, so what I was seeing was presumably the reverse of what an alien would see on the inside. It appeared that the presentation was pre-distorted to compensate for effects due to the curvature of the column.

The Gray enters the cylinder, seats himself, and is automatically strapped in magnetically. He then opens a seam in his suit to expose the port on his lower midriff and connects the umbilical to it. Once connected, the process is initiated via the control buttons on the armrests. The procedure continues until sensors detect that required parameters of nutrition, waste removal, or both have been met. The Gray is then free to exit the enclosure, or stay, thereby utilizing it as a modest crew quarter.

The part of the umbilical that delivers the nutrients is cooled its entire length by a second coaxial tube that constantly circulates refrigerant. The product remaining in the pipeline is maintained at a temperature that keeps it from spoiling. A valve at the connector end automatically prevents spillage and precludes contamination when the tubing is disconnected. While the umbilical is stowed on a mating receptacle on the seat, the material in the pipeline constantly flows through the system. The quality of the product is constantly monitored and remediation is undertaken as needed (adding fluid, controlling the growth of the culture, filtering and culling out corrupted or stale material, etc.).

The waste removal system is under a partial vacuum that assists in conducting waste products away. When stowed, an antibiotic-laced liquid constantly circulates through the system tubing to thwart development of pathogens. The fluid is filtered to remove residual solid matter and is disinfected before being recirculated back to the cubicle. A second and most critical function occurs during periods of interstellar travel when crewmembers, of necessity, must be held in a state of suspended animation for a very long period of time. Occupants of the cubicles are maintained in a state of consciousness amounting to hibernation induced via drugs combined with their nutrient source and by control of the constituents of the atmosphere within the chamber. This state of suspended animation overcomes the harmful physiological effects of extended weightlessness and significantly slows ageing. The Grays are constantly monitored to assess health status, to receive nourishment, and to receive waste removal processes automatically. On a rotating basis and under computer control, one of the crew is awakened to stand watch. This individual would be free to leave the enclosure, retuning routinely as needed for nourishment or relaxation. Remaining fully conscious is mandatory for the duration of the watch, so the sleeplike option cannot be exercised. It is his responsibility to ensure that the life-support hardware and other ship systems function correctly. After the passage of a predetermined period, this crewmember will return to his enclosure to resume his hibernation and another will be awakened for his turn at watch. There may be times when all members of the crew are awakened simultaneously. This could have a significant psychological benefit and would provide assurance that all are in good health. There may also be routine activities that require participation of multiple members of the crew.

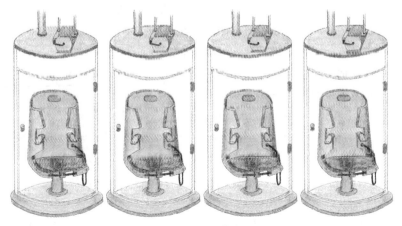

Figure 6: Renewal centers.

During periods other than interspace travel, the need to hook up varies with the individual and the extent of their exertion. The Grays' lifestyle is almost lethargic. They expend very little energy, and their metabolism is appropriately low. The renewal center's life-support system is able to constantly monitor waste product accumulation and bloodstream nutrient and gas levels. Respiration products are assessed in the closed environment of the chamber. Additionally, there is a system similar to the oxygen-measuring finger probes found in our doctor's offices. An alien simply clamps the device on a finger to monitor essential bodily function parameters.

The atmosphere within the renewal chamber is controlled and the ratio of the gasses is adjusted depending on circumstance. During the hibernation period, the level of oxygen is reduced in that the inhabitant's metabolism is radically lowered, and also to conserve a vital commodity.

The Grays' digestive system, such as it is, is unique. It consists of a rudimentary stomach and large and small intestines. Their stomach is primarily vestigial in that the nutrient product they receive can be considered predigested. They have an esophagus and could probably take liquids by mouth; they have no need for teeth. I wondered if there ever was an occasion when they might actually ingest their nutrient gunk orally. Whether they possess the faculty of taste, and if they do, whether the stuff would be pleasing if they were to eat it, is a good question. Their nutrient intake port interfaces the stomach directly. The Gray's rudimentary kidneys are functional. Their urinary output is routed into their colon where it combines with solid waste; the colon then terminates in the surgically added port. The nourishment medium is so effective and their digestion so efficient that little bulk waste is produced. The Grays can go for long periods without the need to expel solid matter.

Waste material is screened for undesirable pathogens and chemical imbalances using sensitive specialized detectors. Status is reported via indicators on both master and renewal center display facilities. Remediation when needed is carried out by the introduction of the appropriate chemical compounds or nutrients under precise machine control.

Water, a precious commodity, is collected from the waste. Compounds used to support the generation of oxygen in the ship's biomass system are also removed and conserved. Before being discharged into space, what remains of the waste matter is burned to reduce mass and to kill any pathogens, and the resultant carbon dioxide gas is collected and stored.

R & R

During terrestrial visits, much of the Grays' time is taken up by routine spaceship maintenance and exploration, collection of samples, and documentation of findings. Still, they have downtime and ordained periods of relative idleness.

The Grays don't have established sleep and wake times, nor do they require simulated daytime and nighttime. When not in the travel mode, crewmembers routinely and at will enter the renewal centers where they can elect to enter a state of extreme relaxation that suffices for sleep.

When not in hibernation, the Grays require exercise to maintain what limited muscle mass they have. An exercise machine resembling a miniature exercise bicycle is deployed for use from an out-of-the-way stowed position. Because this activity is usually conducted during periods of weightlessness, the alien is held in place by a magnetic restraint similar to that of the renewal center seats. A finger probe, also similar to that found in the renewal centers, monitors the physiological effects of the exertion and prompts an indication on the machine's control panel when requisite parameters have been met. This is virtually the only exercise these guys get. The machine is shared among the crew and is used routinely and when health monitoring systems indicate the need.

The Grays require mental stimulation to keep their edge. This is provided by telepathic exchanges in computer-generated number puzzles, games of strategy, and other thought-provoking exercises. Whether the Grays play competitively against one another is unknown.

Also unknown is whether the aliens derive any gratification from accomplishment of any task or exercise and if any activity is carried out just for fun.

It's doubtful that the Grays engage one another socially. We humans have diverse interests and life experiences that are worthy subjects for communal intercourse: in olden days around the fire, in later times on the phone, and these days by email and texting. The Grays have had the same exact shared experience all their lives. Other than exchanges prompted by work necessity, there would be very little to talk about. In fact, the very structure of their spacecraft precludes communal gathering. There just isn't the space or any seating for the Grays to gather other than in the cockpit. The renewal centers impose a deliberate form of isolation. Of course, the crew could engage one another telepathically while in the renewal centers. It just doesn't seem to be in the aliens' nature for Bud in his cubicle to inquire of Burt in his, "How's it going in there?"

So, sitting around shooting the bull verbally or telepathically to foster comity or as a form of relaxation is pretty much out of the question.

Sweat and Toil

Alien hygiene isn't much of a problem. Because for most of their existence the Grays are in a state of suspended animation in a closely temperature-controlled environment, they don't perspire during these periods. At destination, when alert and functioning, and particularly when engaging in routine-prescribed exercise, aliens could exert to the point of perspiring. Life-support system control of the whole ship's ambient temperature and humidity tends to preclude this, however. Bathing is certainly out of the question due to limited resources. Odor-causing bacteria, and for that matter any undesirable bacterial life-form, is continuously removed from the atmosphere by electrostatic filtering equipment. Lacking some of the body components responsible for odor, the aliens are probably never stinky. And, even if they were, they most likely lack olfactory function anyway.

The Grays' spacesuits could conceivably become soiled, especially during terrestrial activities, although the suit's composition tends to repel accumulation of contaminants. Bringing earthly dust, pollen, and dirt aboard the saucer would be big trouble in their environment, especially during times of weightlessness. Although the ship's atmospheric filtering system is effective, unusual soiling can be removed in the renewal centers, which are equipped with an electrostatically charged forced air system to remove and filter out contaminants.

Talk to Me

The Grays communicate with one another telepathically. In my experience they never communicated orally and may lack a functional tongue and vocal cords. The range over which they can communicate telepathically is impressive. They don't have to be within sight to communicate effectively. Attempts at telepathic communication with humans are a different matter. The range is very short and is enhanced greatly by eye-to-eye contact. The mechanism is probably a wavelength of light not visible to us, which is able to stimulate our optic nerve when reflected from the Grays' eyes. The optic nerve would thereby act as the conduit into our, pardon the pun, gray matter. The information is probably conveyed by means of modulating or varying the intensity of the reflected light carrier wave. The process is almost certainly one-way in that we probably lack or haven't discovered and exploited what may be an innate facility to talk back optically. Our responses would thus be telepathic and wouldn't benefit from the enhanced precision of the optical regime.

The Grays transmit thought patterns, suggestions and, most effectively, visualization. Human interpretation of alien thought transfer is at best sketchy even with eye-to-eye contact. We aren't good at it. Comprehension often requires multiple iterations of thought transfer and feedback. Humans are able to initiate communication, but from my experience, the Grays tend to ignore it. (It should be noted that telepathic communication with an implant in place is very concise and visualization is dreamlike but vivid.)

The aliens don't use and are not conversant in human language. They don't listen to our radio stations or watch our TV. What they know of us comes from years of information obtained via telepathic interviews with us and their investigation of our planet's geography, geology, and diverse life-forms. (Study of Earth's life-forms may very well result in the occasional mysterious discovery of surgically dismembered wild and domestic animals.)

The Grays are able to telepathically control machinery that is provided with the appropriate interface. For this they wear headgear that converts thought patterns to machine code. It's possible that control could be exerted without the need of the headgear. But for critical functions such as operating and navigating the ship, the enhanced reaction time and precision that is achieved with the helmet is warranted.

Calling Home

Although travel time from the home base to a planet of interest is very long, the crew aboard the spaceship is virtually unaware of the passage of time. While in their hibernation state, the Grays age very slowly. When they awaken and emerge from the renewal centers to begin their terrestrial exploration, they are only vaguely aware that they've been cooped up for such a long period. Time takes on much greater significance when the Grays are awake and conducting their business.

Meanwhile, the alien masters back on the home planet are presumably awaiting results from the mission. And they could have to wait a long time. Let's assume the alien explorers plan to poke around here and their home planet is twelve light-years away. With an acceleration time of a year or so, then a slow-down time of yet another year, and traveling at the stupendous maximum velocity of 60 percent of the speed of light, the Grays would have been traveling over twenty-two Earth years just getting here. Now, let's suppose that they transmit data back home via radio or laser or anything limited by the speed of light. That's another twelve years the folks back home would have to wait to hear from the probe. So, an aggregate of thirty-four Earth years would have passed. That's a long time to wait, even for a species whose lifetime is very long compared to ours.

They almost certainly don't use cosmic snail mail (radio or lasers) to communicate with their home base. The time a message would take to wing its way through the enormity of outer space over the distances involved would be untenable. Presumably they use real-time techniques such as telepathy or the science of quantum mechanics to circumvent the speed of light limitation.

The Grays may use a variant of the effect known as quantum entanglement to communicate instantaneously between the ship and home. In quantum entanglement, under certain circumstances, two photons generated simultaneously can experience a remarkable effect: what is done to one photon locally immediately happens to the other, potentially located far apart from the first. Einstein referred to it as "spooky action at a distance." Even more bizarre is the associated theory that the process of observing an event actually alters it. Scientists have statistically proven that anticipation of the outcome of an experiment can actually skew the result in that direction. This revelation smacks of often-dismissed claims of telekinesis where people purport to be able to move objects or bend spoons through thought. Debunkers might want to reconsider their negative bias in light of recent scientific finding. Technologists are just now beginning to apply quantum mechanics to computer design with promising potential for radically enhanced capabilities. The Grays most likely have already been there and done that.

Of course, it's possible that the folks on the home planet are endowed with such extraordinary patience that they're willing to accommodate the delay imposed by primitive electromagnetic communication. Or, in the extreme, they might be willing to wait for a ship to return to recover the data and material collected by the crew. And that brings up an interesting question. The Grays do indeed collect physical samples for investigation. Either they are fully equipped to analyze this material and report their findings or the home base is expecting to eventually get custody of the stuff. And if the latter is the case, either they have to wait a long, long time or maybe the Grays have a means of reducing physical items to their basic subatomic constituents and precisely mapping their location so as to transmit the information through space and accurately reconstitute the material at the receiving end; a transporter, if you will. Being able to do this at all would be a monumental breakthrough. Doing it while somehow overcoming the speed of light limitation would be phenomenal, and transporting living things by this means would be an amazing feat. (See "Beam Me Up" in chapter 15.)

The Grays weren't forthcoming on this issue and may purposely have been protecting a unique medium that they don't want us to know about.

Crew

There were three Grays comprising the crew of this spaceship. Oddly, there are four renewal stations. Obviously three aliens are fully able to conduct business, but then why the four cylinders? There are two seats in the cockpit area, which might suggest that a crew of two aliens is the absolute minimum needed. Could the extra Gray be just another example of redundancy for mission survivability?

As mentioned earlier, during the long periods of travel, the crew with the exception of one individual is connected to a life-support system and is maintained in a state of suspended animation. The appointed Gray stays conscious to deal with ship functions that may require attention.

Normally the watch is conducted from the cockpit area where the necessary instrumentation is provided. During periods of acceleration and deceleration where the g-force effects on the occupants are an issue, the Gray on watch must remain in his renewal center. Having to stay alert while locked into the renewal enclosure's seat must be unpleasant. The life-support computer orchestrates watch intervals that rotate often to equitably share the misery. Also, it's very likely that pharmaceuticals are administered to diminish the discomfort without affecting consciousness.

The explorers are probably not expected to return to their home base. The Grays and their ship would thus sadly be considered expendable. Crewmembers will eventually expire. How that situation is dealt with, and what happens when the crew size falls to a point where the mission can no longer continue is a mystery. Do the saucers have an end-of-life destruct provision? Are they programmed to return to the home planet with their deceased occupants when the mission ends? Are there defunct saucers with dead aliens aboard floating around the cosmos?

The life and death issue brings up the question of religious belief. We humans appear to be content with the prospect of death due to the almost universally espoused promise of life after death and the expectation of commune with deceased relatives. Whether the Grays are concerned about their ultimate demise or are predisposed by training to disregard it (World War II Japanese kamikaze pilots for example), or if they are also given to believe in a form of afterlife is unknown. They were probably aware of my desperate spate of praying but never acknowledged it, nor did they exhibit any hint of religious conviction over the course of my association with them.

There is certainly a hierarchy of rank within the crew. It was obvious in my association with the Grays that one of them was the boss. It's possible that the position rotates among the crew, as does the watch responsibility.

As pointed out earlier, the aliens' relationship to one another is far from comradery, being that of workplace interaction and not much more. Because they're genetically engineered specifically for their mission and don't have parents as such, and have undergone intense and highly focused training, they've never experienced the concept, relationships, and benefits of a family. They almost certainly don't possess the emotions associated with love, friendship, or kinship. They can, however, manifest disdain as I unfortunately discovered.

Unlike our astronauts who may possess special skills and training (geology, medicine, earth science), individual crew members have no particular expertise, nor do they need any. Just as my implant afforded me intuitive understanding of some concepts that were clearly beyond my unaided comprehension, likewise is the Grays' ability to cherry-pick the mental acuity needed for a specific task. With their refined telepathic ability, aided by dedicated headgear, they simply download whatever cognition is needed directly into the appropriate region of their brain from a program archived in an onboard computer. Once the task is complete, the Gray can either retain the imported knowledge or elect to forget (essentially clear) the downloaded information.

Home Base

The human conception of home is of a comfortable, welcoming place one returns to by choice following a necessary separation. The Grays have no such luxury; they'll probably never be able to go back home.

The concept of home is probably foreign to the Grays anyway. If they have any recollection of their planet of origin, it's probably as the place where they received training for their life's purpose. The relatively short time spent on the home planet would be of little significance given the long duration of their intergalactic travel.

Where they're from was not disclosed to me. The planet or solar system might have a name in the aliens' parlance that would mean little to us. Their home system is probably identified on our celestial charts and might be familiar if pointed out. Some authorities have claimed that they hail from the binary star system Alpha Centauri, our closest celestial neighbor at a distance of 4.2 light-years. Could be. Due to the limitation on the velocity that their ship can attain while propelled through space, it's reasonable to assume their home planet is probably within a range of 5–50 light-years from here. Considering that the disk's maximum travel rate is at best on the order of 60 per cent of the speed of light, the journey time would seem totally untenable to a species like us, with a life expectancy of seventy-five or eighty years. But what if we could live three hundred, four hundred, five hundred Earth years or more? Time would have a radically different significance. Our biological or circadian clock would run much slower. Time-related urgency and expectation would be proportional to our extended lifetime. The implications of the passage of time to some species of whale and shark for instance would have much less significance than it would to a house mouse whose lifespan is two-hundred times shorter. The Grays experience a life expectancy that is many times our own. The pace of their lives is perfectly in tune with long periods of nothing much happening in their tin can of a spaceship while the cosmos whizzes by. Hopefully they're immune to the concept of boredom during their mandated periods of consciousness.

Gray Wayfarers

At this point it might be instructive to consider a possible relationship between the Grays' penchant for cosmic exploration on a grand scale and circumstances involving their home planet. Prerequisites for a society to successfully undertake intergalactic travel would include a culture fostering a robust scientific inquisitiveness, abundant material and financial resources, a well-educated and intellectually astute population, the luxury of an extended period of societal and political stability, and the time to evolve the appropriate technology. Their spacecraft and its machinery exemplify a well-established industrial capability. For their society to have thus evolved, one would presume that the aliens either conquered or never experienced the perils to long-term survival that we humans face: political instability and wars, religious rebellion, the nuclear weapons threat, environmental devastation, natural or provoked climate change, overpopulation, disease, famine, squandered natural resources, and dwindling raw materials. Being free of those sociologic pressures, having the wherewithal to do the science and the means to produce the hardware, it seems almost inevitable that advanced intelligent beings would bow to curiosity and opt to explore the cosmos.

Then again, there may have been a more compelling and urgent impetus than mere scientific interest for the aliens to undertake interstellar travel.

It is quite possible that the alien society didn't manage their resources well or some natural calamity befell them, or they may have messed up their environment. Perhaps their apparent concern over our development and use of nuclear weapons was born of their own unfortunate experience. These or other exigencies may have prompted the need to abandon their former world to populate a virgin planet, thereby saving their race from impending extinction. The technology developed to relocate scores of inhabitants to this new world could have eventually been turned to interplanetary exploration after the transplanted society became firmly established and comfortable in its new home. If relocation was prompted by some sort of catastrophe, the aliens presumably instituted measures to avoid a recurrence. Alternatively, they could elect to use up the resources or otherwise defile the new planet and then move on. It is reasonable to wonder if mankind will have the luxury of time needed to advance to the Grays' level of sophistication given the many perils we face.

chapter twelve
NUTS AND BOLTS

Here's where we get to dig into the extraterrestrials' technology and hardware. As an engineer, this is the stuff that I find to be fascinating, and this is the stuff that's typically missing from other published accounts.

I knew from observation during my time aboard the Grays' ship that there were many things I longed to know more about. I jotted down topics of interest in my notebook during contemplation after the second visit. I knew, for instance, that computers of some sort were pivotal to the operation of the ship. The Grays obviously had sophisticated propulsion and navigation systems. Their life-support systems and other crucial hardware were of great interest, as was whatever means the aliens instituted to circumvent failure.

I found that if I chose a specific topic, I could mentally access details, as in the commonly accepted analogy of peeling an onion. Details on the outside were sparse and vague. As I worked through each stratum, peeling away layers of the conceptualized onion, the information gleaned became more involved and my mental interrogation became more focused. At each step the responses received via the hardware in my nose were increasingly concise and sharp. At some point in the process, I usually realized that any further digging just yielded information that was beyond my comprehension. During these sessions, I was at first armed with just the notebook into which I feverishly entered data. The process became much more efficient when it dawned on me to dictate into a cassette recorder.

Home Away from Home

In our experience, the word "spacecraft" usually denotes a temporary vehicle for getting astronauts from here to a celestial destination and back again. It's typically meant to support a mission of a few days to perhaps months, as would be the case in a Mars mission. The bottom line: when the mission is over, the astronauts come home, and the crew capsule ends up in a museum somewhere.

Manned Earth-based space missions must carry sufficient expendable materials to last for the duration of the mission. Unexpected loss of critical supplies (Apollo 13) dooms the mission to failure and could very well result in tragedy. In the case of our space stations, consumable supplies and replacements for defective or outdated hardware items are replenished as needed by periodic launches of resupply payloads. Alien explorers, who don't have the luxury of such measures, avoid the intractable problem of needing to store vast quantities of supplies by clever innovation.

The Grays' ship is more a mobile space station than a spacecraft. It has to support a mission lasting many Earth years. It provides all the tools needed for the mission: inexhaustible or renewable fuel, power, and life-support materials including food, water, and air, provides for crew health, safety, and comfort, and has the wherewithal to manage any predictable or unforeseen contingency. Consumable gasses and liquids are collected from a terrestrial environment or mined in space or are created from renewable onboard sources. Often the waste products of one system serve as an input to another. Other ingenious methods promote total self-sufficiency.

The Grays' spacecraft is pretty much all business. The normally stowed small worktable with its associated seat suffices as a repair station and workshop. For big jobs involving repair work on heavy or large items, the infamous examination table can be pressed into service.

The ship affords the barest minimum of creature comforts. The renewal centers offer the only privacy a crew member can find and that is limited to ordained periods of occupancy. In the case of a medical issue requiring quarantine or recovery time, or a physical disability due to a mishap, the individual would no doubt be confined, willingly or otherwise, to one of the renewal centers serving as a hospital room. Presumably another crew member would function as a doctor or nurse, administering whatever treatment was warranted.

Having never experienced luxurious surroundings would be a virtue to the aliens in that there would be nothing to compare their Spartan digs against. This is virtually the only living space the inhabitants will ever know, and it will probably eventually become their tomb.

Failsafe

For the mission to succeed, in theory no critical item can ever fail to function. This means extraordinary planning, sophisticated engineering, enlightened application of materials, and meticulous care during manufacture. It also means strict adherence to routine preventive measures, care in use and handling, innate tolerance of mishaps, etc. And even then, everything has a limited lifetime and will ultimately fail. Ideally anything that breaks down must be repairable. It is of the highest priority that catastrophic failure or degradation to the point of unacceptable performance is ether prevented or can be overcome.

The ship must have the resources aboard to remedy any failure that could ever occur in an essential component. Of course, it would be impossible to stock every vulnerable part. The Grays have developed clever alternatives. The first is component redundancy. Where possible, machines of diverse function use exactly the same component parts, in some cases at the sacrifice of efficiency or size. The other alternative is brilliant: the alien equivalent of 3D printing. Archived computer programs control an onboard machine that can produce a large assortment of mechanical components using a variety of stocked raw materials used in the device as the "ink." Substances used in the fabrication of shipboard equipment were chosen to support the reproduction of parts by this method.

A troubleshooting guide and plan for remediation must be provided for every possible contingency. That amounts to a lot of computer code. As mentioned earlier, the crew has the facility to telepathically receive computer-generated mental stimulation containing pertinent information and instructions. The crew must also have the tools and equipment, resourcefulness, creativity, and intelligence to correctly identify a problem and to marshal whatever is needed to resolve an issue.

There are shipboard systems that due to their nature, complexity, potential health hazard, or inaccessibility cannot be repaired. Should any of these fail, the jig is up. Irreparable critical systems include the nuclear power source, many components of the propulsion system, and some parts of the biologic oxygen generator. Most structures on the outside of the craft are also irreparable as the Grays have no facility for extravehicular forays. These systems have built-in redundancy and are over-designed to tolerate deterioration due to aging, and to survive various forms of calamity. A few hull-mounted items critical to navigation and propulsion are accessible from inside the ship and in most cases repair or replacement is possible, often at the cost of considerable effort.

Protection and Welfare

Obviously, a primary requirement for the spaceship is the well-being of the crew. This includes protection of the crew from external hazards, particularly at velocities attained in interstellar travel. Dangerous elements encountered include thermal and nuclear radiation and micrometeorites. In all three cases, it is the hull of the craft that provides protection. The hull material is a composite of many layers of different materials, some of which contribute to shielding from radiation that occurs due to energetic particle bombardment of the hull. The exterior of the hull becomes very hot; an enormously effective insulating layer prevents the heat from reaching the ship's interior. Other components of the hull sandwich provide a self-healing function meant to prevent penetration into the interior of the craft by a solid particle, the largest of which would measure a small fraction of an inch. In the very unlikely case of penetration through the hull, the escaping atmosphere reacts chemically with specific layers of the composite hull to immediately seal the breach.

A collision with an inordinately large chunk of space debris could result in a rupture of the hull that wouldn't self-heal. If this were to occur, the occupants would have to flee to temporary safety in the renewal centers (if they weren't already there), which provide protection against complete decompression and are equipped with an emergency oxygen source. At least one of the centers has a spacesuit stowed in a locker at the inside top of the structure. Repairs would be made from within the saucer by the appointed crewmember protected by a spacesuit. The wherewithal to seal reasonably sized holes in the hull is anticipated in repair facilities available to the crew. The pressure differential between what air remains in the saucer and the vacuum outside aids in forcing a pliable temporary patch onto the opening, effectively sealing the hole. Once the loss of the ship's atmosphere is staunched, a permanent repair can more leisurely be undertaken.

A massive breach larger than the repair kit could accommodate or the loss of the ship's pressurization before the occupants could reach safety would tragically end the mission.

The Grays' attire affords a unique level of protection. Episodes have been reported of idiotic Wild West mentality shoot-first incidents where aliens have been fired upon by gun-toting humans. In most cases the alien was bowled over by the force of the projectile but was otherwise unharmed. Their suit, which is normally very compliant, is designed to stiffen at impact, safely distributing the bullet's energy over a large surface area much as a policeman's bulletproof vest does. Although it's unlikely that the feature anticipates gun-happy humans, it prevents injuries from mishaps and collisions that could occur in a weightless environment.

Crew Quarters

The ship is both workplace and home to the crew. During interstellar travel, all of the operational functions including life support and navigation are fully automated.

As stated earlier, one member of the crew remains alert during this period and can intervene in ship functions to a very limited extent. In port (i.e., when the craft is under the influence of a celestial body's gravity), navigation is under control of one or two of the Grays from the cockpit of the craft.

The living space is taken up predominately by the renewal centers, machinery, storage tanks, and storage cabinets. There is a small workstation table equipped with a stool that can be deployed from a stowed position. A single larger table is centrally located. A benign purpose could be for surgery in the unlikely occurrence of crewmember illness. A more sinister alternative, and from my experience a very possible one, is the surgical investigations quite often reported by supposed abductees.

What suffices very minimally as crew quarters are the renewal centers discussed earlier. They are just wide enough in circumference to accommodate an alien and provide the only seating on the craft other than in the cockpit section, the exercise machine, and the workstation stool. The normally clear walls of the enclosure can be turned opaque by the occupant if desired. The air temperature within the chamber can be adjusted as can the intensity and even the color of the lighting within the column. While the barest of bare quarters, they do offer a degree of solitude—and are the place where the Grays can go for rest and recuperation.

The seats in the renewal centers are padded and would likely be quite comfortable for casual relaxation. Their utility is much more significant during the long periods of interstellar travel. They provide restraints needed to prevent the alien, who is in a deep sleeplike state, from inadvertent movement that could be harmful. The applied pressure also assists in reducing g-force during acceleration and deceleration. In addition to the magnetic seat belt, the seats are outfitted with two balloon-like airbags that are deployed to gently apply force against each side of the occupant's chest. Armrests are fabricated from a soft rubberlike substance. Rubbery wrist straps are provided. The armrests have push-button switches that control renewal center functions. Two leg restraints are also employed. These are comprised of a soft, pliable material. The chair has notched areas backed with soft, compliant cushions that assist in passively immobilizing the alien's legs. An alert Gray could easily escape the traction although the appropriate computer command can automatically release the bonds.

The two air bags and leg restraints can apply differential pressure to opposite sides of the seated alien, causing his comatose body to shift position. This would at first appear to be a useful tactic in avoiding blood clots that can occur from long periods of inactivity. Because the occupant is weightless during extended periods of travel, the function would seem to be of dubious utility. Maybe there is another purpose that's not obvious to me.

The aliens have very limited space for personal items and very little need for them as well. They don't have mementos such as photographs, rings, and keepsakes because they lack the emotional makeup to treasure such things. Articles used for routine grooming like nail clippers (if they were to actually use them) would probably be communal.

The Grays have the medical stores to handle mishaps such as cuts and abrasions. The ability and resources to treat serious medical emergencies is very limited. Considerable effort is made in the direction of preventative measures to avoid disease or disability. Communicable disease would be highly unlikely. The bugs that would be responsible just don't exist in that closed environment. Bodily functions can, however, falter and even fail. Although the incidence is very rare, the aliens can become ill and can expire as a result.

The only devices remotely resembling video screens are small components evident on the few control panels scattered around, so Grays don't appear to use TV-like appliances for entertainment. Because of their refined telepathic capabilities, it's entirely possible that entertainment is provided through that medium and the option to tap into archived media may be available in the renewal centers.

Time is crucial to many functions of the spacecraft. It is measured in increments that were probably derived from the rotation of the home planet relative to its sun(s) just as ours is. The master clock is a unit that, as far as I can ascertain, functions in a manner similar to our highly stable and accurate atomic clocks. The Grays don't wear wristwatches. They have an innate appreciation of matters pertaining to time. Their built-in circadian clock can be telepathically recalibrated and updated as needed.

Life Support

The life-support system is a complex closed-loop mechanism, involving many intertwined subsystems. The only external inputs to the system are hydrogen, heat, and artificial sunlight.

The atmosphere consists of nitrogen and oxygen. Carbon dioxide (CO_2) generated by alien respiration is removed by scrubbers for storage in pressurized tanks. Unlike the oxygen that is consumed in alien respiration, the nitrogen almost never requires replenishment unless an unlikely penetration of the hull was to allow the atmosphere to escape. Reserve nitrogen can be liberated in a chemical reaction from nitrogen-rich minerals in storage. Further reserves are stored in a tank under high pressure. Between the two sources, there is sufficient nitrogen to replenish the entire volume of the spacecraft a few times.

Oxygen is produced in large enclosed devices whose interior construction resembles the many tiers of a beehive. Layers of biomass convert carbon dioxide piped into the enclosure into oxygen. Nutrients collected from alien waste, water, and artificial sunlight support the process. The output gas contains both oxygen and carbon dioxide. The CO_2 is removed by a dedicated system for recycling, leaving nearly pure O_2.

Water for life support is obtained from terrestrial sources when available and is purified by distillation. When traveling in space, water is produced in machines that burn hydrogen in an oxygen atmosphere. Hydrogen is obtained from specialized collectors on the exterior of the spacecraft. Hydrogen exists in outer space in quantities averaging an atom per cubic centimeter. That doesn't seem like much, but for a spacecraft traveling at 30–60 percent of the speed of light, a lot of hydrogen is encountered; some of the gas collected is liquefied and stored in tanks under high pressure.

Heat is a byproduct of power generation and propulsion systems. Obtaining adequate warm air isn't a problem; removal of excess heat requires the alien equivalent of a large air conditioner to maintain a comfortable environment.

The Grays' nutrient slurry food source is produced in totally automated equipment that grows the culture in a water-based medium in a temperature-controlled environment. Most of the output product is routed to a storage tank that is temperature controlled to allow modest growth of the product. Gasses produced are processed to preserve useful components, mainly

CO_2. A small proportion of the slurry is retained to keep the culture viable. Dehydrated starter culture is stored against the unlikely deterioration of the living culture.

Alien waste is processed in yet another system. Filters remove water that is purified and then committed to storage tanks. Specific components of the solid material are salvaged. The remaining material is heated, and liberated carbon dioxide is collected and stored for use in oxygen generation. The remaining ash is decontaminated and is eventually discharged into space.

It should be noted that while visiting Earth, or any other planet having a similar atmosphere, all essential gasses and water can be easily replenished, allowing the visits to continue indefinitely.

Propulsion

Were it not for the development of a means of propelling a spaceship at velocities approaching or exceeding half the speed of light, the Grays would probably be an unknown backwater civilization. Their propulsion system is the key to their ascendency as cosmic explorers.

Just how effective the Grays' propulsion system is can be appreciated by comparison with our familiar Saturn V launch vehicle. Used to break the bonds of earthly gravity to launch the Apollo moon lander, the expendable three-stage, liquid-fueled rocket was a monster. At a height of 363 feet, it weighed over 6 million pounds with onboard fuel and the 63,500-pound Apollo 11 command and lunar module payload. The Grays' spaceship had to overcome terrestrial gravity on its own when launched and has to surmount our gravity while here: it has no expendable additional launch vehicle. If the space shuttle or today's satellite launches and space station resupply missions had this capability, a lot of cost would be saved and valuable resources that are consumed, abandoned to float around in space, or burn up on reentry would be conserved.

The primary power source aboard the ship is a compact nuclear reactor fueled by a radioactive material, which takes a very long time to decay to its half-life potency. It is of the fission type in that even the aliens with their technological superiority haven't been able to tame nuclear fusion for small efficient power supplies.

The propulsion system, which operates on the principle of matter-antimatter annihilation, requires impressive amounts of electrical power. It uses hydrogen gas as fuel from two sources: one in the proximity of a planet at the start and terminus of travel, and the other in deep space. The hydrogen is converted to antimatter and reacts with matter ambient to the spacecraft to produce the propulsive force. The concept is neat. When the greatest propulsive force is needed (i.e., when the spacecraft is under terrestrial gravitational force and encounters atmospheric friction), the fuel source is abundant. When in space, where gravity is diminished and atmospheric friction is virtually nonexistent, the scant fuel source is still sufficient to generate a strong propulsive force.

In circumstances where substantial bursts of power are needed for abrupt changes in the ship's velocity or direction, electrical energy generated by a large flywheel supplements that of the nuclear reactor. The flywheel's centrifugal force is also harnessed to aid in producing the astounding lightning-fast acceleration and maneuvering agility observed in alien spacecraft.

It should be noted that there has been a lot of discussion on the internet about alien development of antigravity propulsion. Such a system would have a number of virtues. Step function acceleration to extraordinary velocity in seconds should be possible. As with antimatter drive, intergalactic travel speed approaching the speed of light would also be possible. If the ability to control the effects of gravity within the spacecraft could be realized, the deleterious effects of extreme acceleration and deceleration on the crew could be reduced or eliminated.

One technique mentioned online is said to use highly radioactive element 115 (Moscovium) as the power source. Earthbound scientists have only been able to produce a few atoms of the stuff, which has a very short half-life. Speculation is that the aliens have purportedly mastered the generation, containment, and utilization of the element for their antigravity drive.

You'll find more on the topic of antigravity drive in chapter 15, Myth-ed by a Mile.

Waterpower

When navigating in the Grays' home atmosphere, and while in ours, the craft is fueled by water. Water vapor ranges from a trace to around 4 percent of Earth's atmosphere, and presumably at least that amount on the Grays' home planet.

Bulk water collected from the atmosphere and drawn off from terrestrial sources—here and on the home planet—undergoes electrolysis where the hydrogen and oxygen components are produced and extracted. The gasses are compressed and stored in tanks under very high pressure: oxygen as a backup source for the onboard life-support system and hydrogen for propulsion.

The hydrogen gas passes into a reaction chamber where the atom is stripped of its electron, leaving an ion having a proton and a neutron. This undergoes a second processing phase where the neutron is removed, leaving only the proton.

The protons are coerced into two independent beams of highly accelerated particles. The two are then brought together in a magnetic containment vessel such that they smash into each other at tremendous velocity. The result is the generation of antimatter, which is conducted into a second containment vessel where it reacts with elemental hydrogen thereby releasing tremendous additional energy. A portion of the output of this chamber is fed back into the preceding chamber. What results is a bootstrap or regenerative effect that enhances antimatter pro duction, greatly improving overall efficiency and significantly reducing the size of the onboard hardware involved.

After a few passes through both chambers, the antimatter continues to build until the optimum yield is obtained. The quantity of antimatter produced is set by modulating the electrical power applied to the proton accelerating electromagnets ahead of the point where the two beams collide.

There are two identical but independent antimatter generators, each feeding external aft-mounted nozzles located on opposite sides of the ship. Antimatter exits the nozzles where it combines with ambient matter in the space surrounding the saucer in a powerful annihilation reaction of both constituents, thereby producing a strong propulsive force.

The antimatter generators and associated particle accelerators can be visualized as plumbing that wraps a few times around the interior diameter of the ship at its widest point beneath the floor. The apparatus is surrounded the entire length by many contiguous powerful electromagnets and numerous electrically stimulated interior electrodes, each section of which is driven by an independent electronic module. These are located beneath the floor and are accessible via removable flooring panels. Hydrogen protons are accelerated by coordinated computer excitation of the electrodes and electromagnets. Other electromagnets in conjunction with permanent magnets serve to contain the particles within the accelerator. The combination of the bootstrap effect, the unique application of electromagnetic and electrostatic particle acceleration, and the utilization of unusual alloys and other unfamiliar materials results in the achievement of phenomenal performance. Unlike terrestrial particle accelerators that require miles of plumbing (the nuclear research accelerator at CERN on the border of Switzerland and France occupies a tunnel seventeen miles long), each of the Grays' two accelerators if uncoiled would extend only a few hundred feet in linear distance. This is a staggering alien accomplishment.

The craft's velocity and attitude are controlled by the navigational computer. The ship's direction, pitch, yaw, etc. is determined primarily by the antimatter exit angle from the two rear-mounted nozzles, which have four-quadrant freedom of motion, and by differential control of the antimatter output of each generator.

Antimatter must be prevented from any contact with the spaceship's structure. If that was to happen, it would result in catastrophic destruction. The strong electromagnetic force that contains and directs the antimatter exit angle at the port and starboard nozzles assures that annihilation occurs well away from the hull. Nonetheless, numerous safeguards are employed to prevent an occurrence. In particular, sacrificial metal conductors in and around the nozzles that if eroded by antimatter due to a malfunction would immediately cause the propulsion system to shut down.

The nozzles, because of their complexity, are the most potentially failure-prone component of the propulsion system. Due to their criticality, they must be replaceable or repairable from within the spaceship. The task is made difficult in that the nozzles are located in the very confined space where the upper and lower saucer segments comprising the spaceship's hull meet.

A sealed box having an airlock opening and two gloves similar to those of a spacesuit surrounds each nozzle on the inboard side of the ship. To replace a defective nozzle, the Gray first assures that the atmosphere within the box is intact indicating that there is no breach in the seal between the nozzle and the hull. He then opens the small door on an airlock, which is an interface between the ship's interior and an area exposed to the vacuum of space, and puts the replacement nozzle and the tools needed into the box and closes the airlock. With considerable effort, the Gray then executes the replacement using the gloves attached to the box. When the work is complete, the worker opens a small valve, filling the box with the ship's atmosphere. After assuring that there is no leak, the airlock is opened, the defective nozzle and tools are retrieved, and the airlock is resealed.

In the rare circumstance that replacement is needed, the main propulsion system must be shut down. The saucer then either coasts through space or the UFO's unmanned drone's propulsion system can be utilized to maintain the ship's trajectory and velocity. (See "Drone On" in chapter 13.)

When navigating in space, hull-mounted ionic thrusters are used to supplement or trim the propulsion system in influencing the saucer's direction, pitch, yaw, and roll. The ion source is hydrogen atoms that have been stripped of their electron as is done in the first step in the generation of antimatter.

The ionic thrusters are less effective for attitude control in a terrestrial atmosphere. The propulsion system is aided by other thrusters that burn hydrogen in the native oxygen atmosphere (the hydrogen being easily obtained by electrolysis of water), thereby producing a fiery reaction, thrust, and water vapor (steam). These thrusters are particularly helpful in maintaining stability when hovering.

The remarkable ability observed in saucers to almost instantly change course direction is aided by a massive onboard flywheel. By instantaneously changing the rotational axis of the flywheel, the centrifugal force and gyroscopic action assists in propelling the craft in the intended alternate direction.

The propulsion system produces an external field that has strong tertiary effects. It ionizes the air, produces a lot of UV light, and outputs strong wideband electromagnetic energy. It is probably this strong electric field that overwhelmed the electronics of ten Minuteman ICBMs that were purportedly deactivated by a UFO that appeared at a site near Malmstrom Air Force Base in Montana in 1967.

When navigating in the proximity of a planet, the ship is under control of a pilot from the windowed cockpit dome on the top of the craft. The celestial nav system uses star position as a reference and is viable in space until the sky is obscured by sunlight and the atmosphere of the visited planet. Then navigation is up to the crew, aided by laser ranging and sophisticated terrain avoidance systems. Control can be exercised using a joy stick or telepathic input to a navigation system computer.

The propulsion system requires power for containment magnetics that at times of extreme acceleration can exceed the capacity of the nuclear plant. Even with an abundant source of terrestrial water, stored electrical energy is sometimes necessary as an instantaneous supplement to the power plant. The kinetic energy of the flywheel and the associated electrical generator is the source of the needed power boost. Periods of maximum acceleration are thus limited by the stored energy available. The tendency is to get from one place to another rapidly and then assume an operational mode requiring much less power (orbiting in reduced gravity, while landed on the ground, or even underwater), thus facilitating recharging of the energy storage system.

Pedal to the Metal

To begin interstellar travel from a terrestrial starting point, the system is powered by the disassociation of water (electrolysis) to obtain hydrogen. The spaceship then accelerates to the velocity at which the second source of hydrogen can take over. As mentioned earlier, hydrogen exists in space in a density of about one atom per cubic centimeter. That's not much unless you're smacking into those few atoms at a fair percentage of the speed of light—then there's plenty. As the ship's velocity increases and hydrogen collected becomes significant, it supplements the onboard source. When the craft's velocity reaches a threshold where free hydrogen atoms are in sufficient quantity, the spacecraft switches to them as the sole proton source. Needless to say, should the ship's speed fall below a critical threshold where insufficient hydrogen is collected, there would be no way to restart the voyage except for using whatever water remained in storage as the source of hydrogen. That might not be enough.

It would seem counterintuitive that there would be enough matter in the vacuum of space to produce useful thrust in a reaction with the antimatter. The violent annihilation liberates so much energy that the few hydrogen atoms floating around in space provide more than enough matter for propulsion. Hydrogen is thus the fuel source processed to produce antimatter, and hydrogen and other scant atoms existing in space are the reagent.

The conversion of hydrogen atoms to antimatter is inefficient during interstellar travel and requires more power than the nuclear source can provide. At the substantial velocity the ship is able to attain (a fair percentage of the speed of light), the bombardment of free atoms in space produces tremendous heating of the ship's hull. The leading-edge surface of the hull that sustains the greatest heating is outfitted with devices similar in principle to, but much more efficient than, our bimetallic thermocouples. Interconnected, these devices generate the balance of electric power needed for the containment and acceleration magnets of the particle accelerators. Once reaching operational velocity, the ship is oriented in attitude to optimize production of the supplemental power and to a limited extent during periods of acceleration and deceleration. (See "G-force" below.) The velocity of the spacecraft is automatically varied dependent upon the density of particle bombardment to maintain hull heating within predetermined safe bounds. In regions where particle density is high (gas clouds), the ship's velocity has to be reduced substantially.

Hydrogen in space is acquired using two tubelike structures running longitudinally forward to aft on each side of the saucer's hull. The tubes are formed from the same rugged composite material as the hull. Within each tube is a smaller tubular mesh covered in a membrane that reacts with hydrogen atoms in a high temperature catalytic process. Hydrogen passes through the charged membrane into a partial vacuum on the inboard side and is collected in the area between the mesh and the tubes. The longitudinal orientation of the structures and a strong repulsive electric field assures that any particulate matter passes through without contact.

G-force

To avoid exposing the crew to excessive g-forces in periods of acceleration and deceleration, the rate of change in velocity must be limited. During these periods, ramping up to or slowing down from the operational velocity would normally take a very long time. The aliens have developed a way to limit the g-force on the occupants to allow safe acceleration and deceleration at rates of change many times what would otherwise be possible. The attitude of the spaceship is adjusted to minimize the g-force exerted vertically on the aliens' spine while strapped into their chambers or seated in the cockpit. Like us, their spine can be damaged by excessive pressure that tends to compress their vertebrae. In a neat technique to further reduce the effect, the seat in the renewal center can be made to slowly rotate, distributing the g-force evenly across the alien's entire body. An interesting aside: when a Gray exits the column, the command to open the entrance stops any rotation and automatically positions the seat so that it is facing the opening.

When taking off from a terrestrial landing, a saucer is often seen to tilt as it speeds away. This tactic distributes the acceleration g-force on an alien seated in the cockpit or in a renewal center over two axes, greatly reducing the stress incurred. Spectacular rates of climb can be realized without endangering the occupants.

Even considering the schemes to reduce the g-force effect, the ramp-up period to the operating velocity and the ramp-down period from it is still a very significant factor in the overall cosmic travel time.

Claims have been made that alien spacecraft can achieve velocities well in excess of the speed of light. What total bunk! First, there's absolutely no way matter could be accelerated to that velocity. And, even if it could, physical law tells us that the energy needed would be staggering. Secondly, the g-force the inhabitants of such a vehicle would experience would instantly turn them to mush a few nanoseconds before the spacecraft itself vaporized. It has been suggested, however, that there may be ways to get from place to place in space at velocities effectively exceeding the speed of light while the spacecraft itself travels well below that threshold. (See "Warped Concept" in chapter 15.) The Grays have no such capability. Under ideal conditions, the Grays' antimatter propulsion system can achieve velocities of 30–60 percent of the speed of light after a very long period of acceleration. The ability to be propelled through space at this remarkable velocity is an awesome testament to alien tech savvy.

Navigation

Navigation in space is coordinated by an onboard computer.

The ship's velocity is measured by discerning the red shift of a target star lying exactly opposite to the direction of travel. Just as the Doppler effect causes the sound of a passing train whistle to sound lower in pitch as it moves away from the observer, moving away from a light source causes it to appear lower in frequency: a shift toward the red end of the color spectrum. The target star's color temperature (in our parlance blue is cool, red is warm) is first measured at minimum velocity as a calibration point. Subsequent measurements are made during travel to determine the craft's velocity, and antimatter production is adjusted to maintain the required speed.

In deep space, navigation is conducted using input from three systems and sources that can function independently or in concert with one another. One is optical. A star map and pre-plotted course is maintained in the onboard navigational computer. A bright celestial object or a pattern of objects is selected as a reference point and is maintained in the crosshairs of highly directional IR and visible light sensors by appropriate adjustment of the ship's trajectory. The imaging devices face aft. Forward-facing optical sensors would be impossible to protect from the severe particle bombardment encountered in space at close to relativistic velocity.

The optical sensors are supplemented by a highly sensitive and directional X-ray receiver system, whose detectors also face aft. The computer is programmed to augment the craft's course by maintaining a lock on a preselected celestial X-ray source such as a pulsar.

The third source is a microwave receiver system. The ship has four forward-facing dishes (antennas) feeding four independent receivers comprising a phased array system that has much greater sensitivity and resolution than a single receiver. The antennas' reflectors and the active elements called feed horns are comprised of the same rugged hull material that is fully capable of withstanding the rigors of space. A strong celestial noise source (supernova, black hole) is programmed to be monitored. The saucer's track is adjusted to keep the source centered in the receivers' tight directivity pattern in coordination with the optical and X-ray sensors.

The microwave system is considered as a tertiary or backup aid. It is prone to noise interference from the barrage of space-borne particles and the vessel's own propulsion system. Noise due to particle bombardment peaks and ebbs repeatedly as the ship's velocity increases or decreases. At the microwave system's frequency of interest, the effect can be envisioned as a comb, teeth facing upward, with the craft's velocity as the baseline: i.e., the comb's backbone. For this system to be useful, the saucer's velocity has to be adjusted so that interfering interstellar noise falls within one of the comb's null points. A further necessity is to periodically and briefly interrupt the propulsion system when using microwaves as a source of navigational data. An additional complication is the need to vary the receive frequency to compensate for the effect of Doppler shift due to the saucer's approach velocity.

For redundancy, there are numerous optical sensors peering out of small windows comprised of a thick, strong transparent material on the backside of the saucer. The instruments, of which there are many spares and spare components, can be removed and replaced from within the saucer.

Numerous X-ray detector spares and replacement parts are in storage and the units can also be replaced from inside the spacecraft.

The four microwave dishes not only provide redundancy (albeit with reduced effectiveness if any were to fail) but are also used in a highly accurate active radar system that serves as a backup to an onboard light detection and ranging (lidar) system used exclusively when in proximity of a terrestrial destination.

The lidar system is similar in theory and application to radar except that it uses powerful laser light in lieu of radio frequencies. Lidar is used primarily to obtain range information and for terrain avoidance. Its sensors are behind very small forward- and downward-facing apertures in the hull that are automatically covered for protection during interstellar travel. Lidar system components are tiny compared to the radar antennas and support equipment, and there are many spares aboard that can also be replaced from within the craft.

As mentioned earlier, when in a terrestrial environment, an alien can manually fly the spaceship from the cockpit area via a joystick control while adhering to an alien equivalent of what our airline pilots refer to as VFR or visual flight rules.

Controlling the ship manually in space at functional velocity would be impossible for even a Gray. The effort would require constant and intense vigilance and reaction time that only a computer-driven system can accommodate.

A small active phased array sonar system monitors underwater terrain on occasions when the craft is submerged. (See chapter 13: Hide and Seek and the "Jet Ski" section.) The rugged forward-facing piezoelectric transducers that produce the incident sonar signal and receive the reflected return easily withstand the battering of particulate material encountered in space travel. In fact, because each strike produces an electronic signature, the array is monitored to count the hits to assess the density of micrometeorite stuff in the spaceship's path.

Not Your Average Laptop

Obviously every system and subsystem that requires an input whether manual or automatic is addressed through hardware that we'd call a computer. The architecture is far more advanced than ours, but the basic functions can be referred to in terms familiar to our computer technology. Although there are numerous subordinate processors scattered around, there are only three major CPUs aboard the spacecraft. Although interconnected, these central processing units primarily serve the discrete functions of navigation, propulsion, and life support. (Hardware that could marginally be considered a computer is located on the drone.)

The propulsion computer primarily administers the generation of electrical power in the nuclear reactor, the hull-mounted thermoelectric source, and the flywheel. It governs the collection of hydrogen, and with input from the navigation computer, controls the generation of antimatter and its exit angle at the hull nozzles. This computer also manages the production of the ions fed to the ship's thrusters.

The navigation computer archives star maps and other navigation aids, orchestrates autonomous navigation in deep space, handles manual UFO and drone flight control input from the cockpit during terrestrial activities, and manages hull-mounted navigational sensor inputs.

The life-support computer oversees the collection or generation and storage of essential gasses and water, produces and maintains the Grays' nutrition source, manages the recovery of useful constituents from biologic waste, controls the gas content and temperature and humidity of the internal environment, monitors the aliens' health status, is the source of exercises aimed at mental stimulation, manages their hibernation period, and orchestrates communication between the Grays and the implant devices.

The three computers, which are situated in the cockpit area, archive reams of data aimed at maintenance, troubleshooting, and fault remediation. The navigation and propulsion computers control the 3D printer in the production of spare parts.

Considering the Grays' technological superiority, one would expect their computers to be superfast, profoundly intelligent, and tiny. That's not the case. Unlike our laptops and towers that must accommodate a wide variety of applications, the aliens' computers are very focused on their purpose. With the exception of some aspects of navigation, most things being controlled don't require fantastic computer speed; thus, the attendant benefit of cooler and more power-efficient hardware is realized. Likewise, functions performed are for the most part perfunctory. Lots of memory is required, but the need for adaptive intelligence is limited. Size is important in the limited space available, but the primary hardware design goals of accuracy, reliability, and survivability are paramount, even at the sacrifice of other desirable attributes.

Computer hardware is modularized, consisting of five module types that we would classify as power supply, read-only memory, fast processor, slow processor, and input/output interface. No matter where used, the modules of a given type are identical.

The hardware of each discrete computer system is duplicated in triplicate, with all three subsystems performing the very same task in parallel. This includes triple interface paths to controlled or source subsystems. Performance-monitoring algorithms are fully satisfied if all three of these computers return the same answer. The logic will deem two out of three subsystems okay if they return the same result and will flag the errant subsystem as faulty.

The Grays are assisted in troubleshooting the hardware by fault location algorithms that identify failures down to the sub-module level. Spare modules are maintained in storage for use as replacements. The modules themselves are designed to be repairable. They consist of easily replaced subcomponents that are alike insofar as possible, again at a modest sacrifice of size economy.

Application software is archived in optical read-only memory (ROM) modules that are far more sophisticated than our CDs and DVDs. While we've progressed to solid state flash memory devices (SIM cards, thumb drives), the aliens have opted for the long-term reliability afforded by their optical data storage regime. The limited scratchpad memory the computers require is embedded in the processor modules.

The ROM modules consist of a square format medium, four X-Y addressable mirrors, four coherent light sources of two different wavelengths, and two photo detectors. Rather than spin the medium to acquire data using motors and bearings, which are prone to failure in our CD and DVD readers, the Grays' solution is to scan the matrix with coherent light using tiny low-mass mirrors and electromechanical drivers having a very long life expectancy.

The ROM modules have incredible data density. The optical technique employed doubles the storage capacity, and use of both sides of the medium doubles it again. The heart of the module is a sandwich of two optical filters and a reflective surface. The first filter passes red light and blocks blue while the second filter passes blue light and blocks red. At the time of programming, tiny holes are burned by a laser into the first filter allowing blue light to pass through it to the second filter, which passes blue light to the reflective surface. Likewise, during programming, tiny holes are burned into the second filter allowing red light to reach the reflector. Light of either wavelength reaching the reflector is bounced back through the filters to an external photo detector where it generates the equivalent of a binary logic 1 state. Thus, completely independent data are accessible depending upon the wavelength of the incident light. The reflector at the center of the filter sandwiches prevents optical crosstalk between the sides.

The Grays have a limited option to modify software and to author new code. What the Grays generate is tagged as unique and is consigned to dedicated read/write memory sections of the processor modules. The new code can have significant impact on system functions, but only with machine concurrence that safety of flight isn't impacted, and only as subordinate to the original base code.

chapter thirteen
HIDE AND SEEK

Once the Grays arrive at a destination, they plan to stay around for a long while conducting their observations and research. Needless to say, they strive to be undetected in their pursuits. The time they spend in situations where they are vulnerable to discovery is very limited. They breeze in, hastily complete whatever task they're undertaking, and breeze out. Most of the remaining time, they're parked.

Prior to the 1960s, the most clandestine parking site was the far side of the moon where they landed to conserve fuel and were the least susceptible to detection from Earth. That changed during the years of the Apollo missions when the manned service module and lander orbited the moon. The aliens were forced to make other arrangements.

Nowadays there are two parking options in their visits here. The first is to park in an Earth orbit and employ countermeasures that assist in avoiding attention.

They're also able to dock in large lakes and the ocean. The saucer is equipped with hull-mounted barriers that are employed to cover the few external instruments that need protection during a dunking. Although the hull is extremely rugged, the depth of safe penetration is limited to around that of our deepest venturing submersibles.

The craft assumes neutral buoyancy by taking on or expelling seawater from storage tanks dedicated to terrestrial water collection. It can hover in place with minimal expenditure of power.

The only possible risk of exposure is a passing submarine. The saucer is typically far below a sub's operating depth. In the very unlikely occurrence of being discovered, the saucer can speedily exit the water in its typical awe-inspiring manner.

The ocean would constitute a great hiding place or an ideal location for a clandestine alien base of operation as has been suggested by some authors. As much as 80 percent of the ocean floor is unexplored and uncharted. With their spacecraft's virtually infinite resources, the aliens could very well choose to linger for months in a watery hiding place, popping out occasionally to conduct their research.

Jet Ski

The antimatter drive is useless in the water. Although even saltwater won't damage the external propulsion system components, the output nozzles are automatically covered by a water-pressure-activated barrier. The saucer is propelled in the water much as is a Jet Ski. The forward-facing ports used in outer space for hydrogen collection are repurposed to channel seawater into powerful pumps. The pumps output a powerful torrent of water from the also-repurposed aft-facing hydrogen collection system ports. Vanes in the output ports direct the water flow to control the craft's attitude and direction.

The pilot navigates the saucer from the cockpit utilizing the T-handle, joystick, and other controls on the seat and the instrument cluster. Powerful forward-facing lights illuminate the craft's course as observed from the viewports. Underwater terrain avoidance is provided by the phased array sonar system. The hull-mounted sonar transducers are also used to listen in on and study sounds made by ocean-borne biologics such as whales, shockwaves caused by seismic disturbances, and the background roar of ship engines.

The Grays have a limited capability to collect waterborne specimens. A remotely controlled claw is able to grab an item to be studied. The captured article is then dropped into an external basket attached to the ship's hull, and the basket's lid is closed using the claw. To retrieve the item, the ship must exit the water and land so that an alien can remove the temporarily attached basket and carry it and the contents into the spacecraft. The basket is then stowed inside the craft until needed again.

A lot has to happen all at once when exiting the water. First, enough momentum needs to be developed that the saucer will be propelled out of the water. Instantaneously, when the aft portion clears the water, a jet of high-pressure air opens the antimatter nozzle barriers and clears them of residual water. The normal propulsion system is then able to take over. This all happens so fast that the only obvious artifact is a slight wobble often noted by witnesses as a UFO departs the water. Occasionally a loud bang is heard as antimatter explosively annihilates any water remaining in the system nozzles.

Drone On

Lights in the sky and small UFOs exhibiting breathtaking aerodynamic performance reported by some observers are often what we refer to as unmanned aerial vehicles (UAVs) or drones. These remote-controlled, autonomous, pregnant-saucer-shaped vehicles are used for terrestrial surveillance and collection of samples, and to seemingly challenge earthly flying machines for reconnaissance purposes or maybe even for fun. They are much smaller than the mother craft and dock unobtrusively on the underside of the larger saucer.

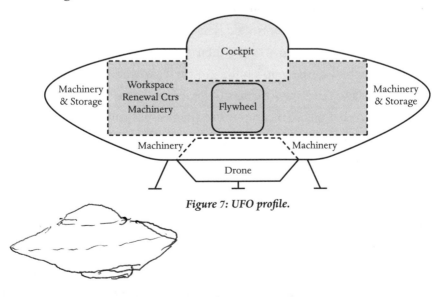

Figure 7: UFO profile.

The drone is propelled by small hybrid electric and hydrogen gas-powered engines reminiscent of our turbofans. The drone's four rotors are principally powered by efficient and potent electric motors. Hydrogen-burning turbines share the same rotor shafts and the turbines and thrusters mounted on the periphery of the craft supplement the electric motors when an extreme change in velocity or direction is warranted. The combination of power sources accounts for the UAV's remarkable hovering capability and extraordinary high-speed maneuverability.

The drone is equipped with imaging sensors in visible light, IR, and UV. The IR instrument detects the presence of anything warmer or cooler than the surrounding environment including animals and people. The UAV has wideband electromagnetic radiation detectors, can collect and analyze terrestrial atmospheric gasses, and senses atmospheric weather-related characteristics. The sensors can be activated with the drone docked, parked, or while roving. When deployed, the UAV can gather and store small samples of solid materials including biologics. Ominously, it has a high-powered laser that can scan a sample, vaporizing it layer by layer while another instrument samples the gasses liberated and analyzes the constituents. The process would obviously be lethal to a biologic subject. The laser can also be used to slice and dice a sample into smaller portions for collection.

While docked on the mother ship, samples collected can be retrieved through mating airlock ports in the drone and the spaceship. Once moored, the drone charges its electrical system from the mother ship and takes on hydrogen, which is committed to tanks aboard the drone and is compressed to extremely high pressure.

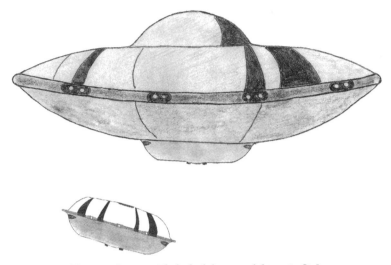

Figure 8: Saucer with docked drone and drone in flight.

Hydrogen is a logical choice as a fuel in that the mother ship produces it via electrolysis of abundantly accessible terrestrial water.

The drone's flight time is limited by its consumable gas storage volume and electrical storage capacity. It returns to the airborne mother craft to recharge when necessary.

When cruising on the electric turbofans, the drone can be reasonably clandestine. During periods of intense acceleration, when the gas turbines and thrusters are used, the UAV has a pronounced IR signature. The turbines are notoriously noisy, a situation that would be untenable in the drone's use for covert investigation. Sophisticated noise abatement techniques are employed with somewhat limited effectiveness. Along with sound-deflecting baffles, powerful transducers that resemble our metallic public address loudspeakers introduce a noise signature that has the same characteristics as that of the engines but is opposite in phase to the turbine whine. Beamed downward, the complementary sound pressure is quite effective in cancelling out engine noise at ground level when the drone is high overhead.

The UFO can be airborne, at least partially submerged, or parked on the ground during a drone mission. Launch and recovery of the drone requires that the UFO be airborne. The drone is controlled by the alien pilot from the mother ship's cockpit. Deployment and operation of the vehicle usually involves two Grays: one to drive the UFO and the other to control the UAV. Navigational feedback is visible via binocular and IR sensors and high-resolution lidar.

Telemetry between the mother ship and the drone is probably a form of quantum communication, although reported behavior of the UFO during drone deployment doesn't rule out the obsolete (to aliens) use of radio. On at least one occasion the pilot of a military aircraft that was in pursuit of a drone reported seeing a large craft parked just below the surface of a nearby body of water. This would make sense if an antenna was in use. Water might interfere with some other form of telemetry as well. Otherwise, for stealth, one would think the mother ship would opt for deeper submersion.

The telemetry received from the drone is converted at the mother ship to a format that is compatible with the aliens' telepathic headgear such that the pilot clearly sees what the UAV's sensors pick up. He can also manipulate the drone telepathically or manually using the joystick and T-handle, or by a combination of both. Information returned can be archived in digital memory.

The exhaust from the drone's turbines can be used to supplement the UFO's propulsion system when an extra boost in performance is required. In this application it consumes precious hydrogen and oxygen. In a terrestrial environment, atmospheric oxygen is used to support the burning of hydrogen in the turbofan engines. In space, O_2 is sourced via plumbing from the saucer; it is not stored aboard the drone. Quantities of gas used are reasonable for short spurts of supplemental propulsion, as the turbine's exhaust, which is essentially steam, is extremely efficient in the vacuum of space.

In addition, in instances where the UFO's main propulsion system is temporarily disabled, the drone can generate sufficient power to maintain the mother ship's operational velocity for very short periods in deep space. Because the UAV would consume substantial quantities of vital gas reserves, it would only be used in response to an emergency situation. The drone would be unable to provide enough power to accelerate the UFO and would be totally ineffective in the presence of planetary gravity.

The UAV can be used to inspect surfaces of the mother ship that would otherwise be difficult to get to. Its hydraulic claw could be used to dislodge terrestrial contaminants like seaweed, leaves, etc. that might adhere to some surfaces and would be beyond the reach of a four-foot alien. The drone's use for maintenance activity in deep space is prevented by the inordinate time required to slow the UFO to a safe launch speed and the uncertainty of being able to resume the mother ship's operational velocity from an idle. (See "Pedal to the Metal" in chapter 12.)

There is virtually no means to affect a repair on a drone if it was to suffer a critical failure. A defunct drone is not considered expendable, however, as its structure completes the hull of the mother ship. The mother ship can function in a situation where a defective drone can't be recovered but the mission would be critically impaired by the loss. Maneuverability in space is unaffected. Turbulence caused by the open docking port in a planetary atmosphere reduces propulsion efficiency.

Accounts have recently surfaced of sightings made in 2004 by navy aircraft of substantially larger objects than the Grays' drone (which also exhibited incredible aerodynamic performance) and were observed to be similar in shape to the candy known as Tic Tacs. I suspect that these are more sophisticated UAVs associated with much larger saucers than the one(s) I encountered.

chapter fourteen
FINGER ON OUR PULSE

Judging from my experience and those documented by others, aside from slicing up a few farm animals and perhaps collecting botanical samples, a primary goal of our galactic explorers is investigating us. In doing so, they're dealing with a species possessing a strong free will and vastly superior physical strength. If they were to elicit our disfavor and it was a fair match, they'd lose. What turns the tables is the Grays' ability to exercise control of a potential human adversary via the aliens' highly developed telepathic capability, which is effective in subjects with or without the infamous implant. Alien domination over humans may also be achieved by other specialized means as well.

We'll explore two very effective weapons in the aliens' telepathic arsenal in this chapter.

The Implant

The implant allows the aliens to monitor human thought patterns and also to stimulate our brain to produce mental images and to instill ideas and notions. Unfortunately, the implant has to be inserted into human flesh in proximity of the brain to be effective.

Because of my implant, I was able to acquire a great deal of information regarding the Grays without needing dialogue with an alien. When a topic of interest presented itself, I instinctively knew the details. The pertinent facts were just there. I strongly believe the implant was tapped into some sort of AI (artificial intelligence) or even an artificial consciousness that was aware and was a source of a vast spectrum of information.

Digressing a bit, the thought of an artificial consciousness brings up an interesting point. Consider the possibility of a repository of all knowledge, a storehouse where all the secrets are kept, a library of everything. Could the Grays have access to such a resource? Is their advancement relative to our own due to their library key being able to unlock more of the files than ours? How could we acquire a better key?

Returning to the topic, the implant is a marvel of compact and efficient technology. The module is partitioned into sections, each with a dedicated purpose.

The skin of the implant is comprised of a material that thwarts the human body's tendency to reject a foreign object. It also prevents vascular and tissue growth that could tend to encapsulate the device. The device's structure is such that it will remain in place but can be removed without undue damage to surrounding tissue.

The unit requires low-level, keep-alive power to maintain activity in the idle circuitry that is provided by the reaction of two dissimilar metals against body chemistry. The metals eventually erode over a period of years, causing the implant to fail. Chemical byproducts produced are not harmful in the small quantities involved. Individuals the aliens wish to surveil beyond the implant's lifetime would have to undergo removal and replacement of the device.

A special section of the implant is sensitive to the human brain's electrical impulses commonly referred to as brainwaves. The detected thought signals are converted to a format that permits transmission to a remote receiving device. Once converted, the information can be accumulated in a committed short-term digital storage area.

The device is, in effect, a transceiver. One area produces the carrier signal used to transmit the data. Another is a receiver of inbound information encoded in the same format as the transmitted data. The recovered signal is routed to a converter that produces the protocol needed to stimulate the brain.

The implant has to be excited by a strong external signal to be effective at long range. While it can initiate transmission of data on its own, it essentially relies on the incoming power as a source of energy for its transmit section to function optimally.

The Grays can recover data from or send data to the device in either a continuous mode or a burst mode.

In the continuous mode, the alien spacecraft has to remain constantly within the relatively short range of the implant. This is a burden undertaken in specific situations, generally short-term, where unbroken communication is essential.

The preferred regime is the burst mode wherein the aliens download or upload the implant's limited on-board memory in one shot or burst. This requires the ship to be within range for a relatively short time.

An alternative solution involves tiny geosynchronous satellites used as relay stations. The satellites, each of which can manage multiple implants, have a repeater mode that greatly increases the range of an implant. Data throughput can be real-time with no memory involved or can be committed to onboard memory. The alien ship would still need to be within range of the satellite but could be a long way off, remaining aloof and clandestine in the effort.

The satellites have substantially larger onboard memory capacity than the implants and can thus monitor and record the implant's data stream for long periods of time. The stored data can be downloaded in a continuous stream or in a burst mode similar to that used to address the implant's memory. The downside is that the information recovered in both modes is old.

The satellites' small size and location amid quantities of space junk make them virtually undetectable. They can be easily deployed but are unrecoverable and are thus expendable; a puff of compressed gas released upon command will propel the satellite out of orbit to a flaming demise in the planet's atmosphere.

Stun Gun

Although this didn't happen to me, I have no reason to doubt reports of people being immobilized by aliens during a confrontation. This could be done as a means of exercising control over

humans who would certainly prevail in a solely physical altercation. It could also be used in a benign way to prevent curious
people from approaching a saucer that's producing potentially
harmful radiation.

The Grays surely possess the ability to overpower people
telepathically at least at short range and through an implant if
the human happens to be so endowed.

There have been reports of people being engulfed in a beam
of blue light emanating from a saucer and finding themselves
instantly unable to move. The implication is that the beam is
somehow able to physically disable and immobilize a person.
While this is a possibility, I believe that the blue beam is a carrier
of information and the effect is more subliminal than physical.
Just as aliens are better able to convey thoughts telepathically
eye to eye, intelligence could be conveyed via the blue light. In
stimulating a person's optic nerve, the data embedded in the
blue light has direct access to the brain and could convey the
appropriate command including instigating loss of muscle control resulting in immobilization. Using this medium, an alien
could instill all manner of commands and suggestions without
even stepping out of the saucer. People who relate details of an
abduction often report first awaking to a room bathed in blue
light. This could be the aliens' means of preconditioning the
abductee to the impending encounter by way of instructions
embedded in the light.

Why blue light? The answer may lie in the propensity of the
short wavelength blue light (between 400 and 525 nanometers)
to penetrate to the back of a person's retina, where it would

more directly stimulate the optic nerve than the longer wave-lengths. Blue light would presumably be a more efficient agent to use as a carrier than other colors. It would be interesting to know if people wearing computer glasses that intentionally block blue light are immune from light-borne alien suggestion.

chapter fifteen
MYTH-ED BY A MILE

In this section, we discuss a few popular notions regarding aliens that have a tinge of myth surrounding them. While not dismissing them all out of hand, they're cited here because facets of the topics tend to be at odds with discoveries I made during my association with the aliens.

Speaking Universally

The universe is huge. Astronomers glibly speak of things millions of light-years apart. Light travels 186,000 miles in a second. That's almost six trillion (6,000,000,000,000) miles in a year. So a celestial object our scientists have discovered at, let's say, nine-hundred-million light-years distant is a long, long way off: in miles that's 5.4 with 21 zeros. But that distance is really just a short hop in the universe that's said to be infinitely large. When we drill down on that concept, it's mind-blowing. In the human experience everything has a size and a boundary. The lamp is on a table in the living room of a house on a street in a town in a county in a state in a country on a continent ... a thing within a bigger thing within an even bigger thing. In an infinite universe, there's no final border, no limit, no edge. We're told the universe started as a fly spec at the time of the cosmic explosion known as the big bang that marked its beginning and has been expanding ever since. But when it was a tiny dot it must have been suspended within something bigger. There had to be a demarcation of where the universe was and where it wasn't, and where it wasn't has to be a different place. A universe within another universe within yet another going on forever? Limitless is hard for the human mind to fathom.

We're certainly not going to solve the quandary here. An infinite universe may not just be unending in size. It could be that in an infinite universe, there's an infinite chance that *anything* can exist, *anything* can happen. There could be multiple Earths with multiple clones of you and me living out various stages of our lives. ESP (extrasensory perception), wherein people sense an event before it occurs, may be a form of crosstalk from what's happening to us at the time on another world. Preposterous? Maybe, but in an infinite universe, what seems to us to be bizarre and unfathomable might just be normal.

The point is, I'm about to declare some conceptions related to aliens as myths. From my vantage point, it's a pretty easy call. But in an infinite universe ...

Alien Federation

We are led to believe from some accounts that Earth's visitors are of many different species. We're told that there is a federation of planets comprised of a diverse collection of alien types engaged in intergalactic exploration. One could envision a group consisting of Grays, reptilians, and praying mantis types sitting around a table, communicating telepathically, planning their next exploit. Emissaries would then be handed their orders and would be dispatched in an assortment of spaceships (saucers, cigar shaped, triangular) to carry out their work and report back to the waiting commission. Why we'd be visited by so many different entities is puzzling when for efficiency it would seem that one commission representative would be enough. There are many worlds out there to investigate. Why gang up on us?

Alien Purpose

Depending upon what you read, the alien visitors have a number of purposes. In some reports they're trying to save us from ourselves as regards the nuclear threat. This could be a valid argument as evidenced by the incident at the air force base at Roswell, New Mexico, toward the end of World War II. Roswell may have been a storage facility for what were at that time primitive nuclear weapons. The saucer that crashed there may have been on a mission to assess the threat to mankind represented by this new weapon. As mentioned earlier, in another case that occurred in the '60s, ten ICBMs at a Montana site were reportedly taken off-line by one or more UFOs observed in the area by military personnel. The problem is, if thwarting our nuclear ambitions was the goal, the effort hasn't been very successful. The aliens have presumably been observing our nuclear foolishness for decades and the bombs and missiles are still with us. To make matters worse, certain belligerent countries are currently bent on developing their own nuclear arsenals. Our cosmic visitors could be helpful here by zapping a few of their centrifuges.

Another rather unlikely supposition is that they're looking for a new planet to colonize. Speculation has been made that their sun is dying and their planet will eventually be uninhabitable. They'd be forced to load up Noah's alien resource conveyance (ARC) with the life-forms they wanted to preserve and head our way. Their interest in us, of course, would be to keep mankind from messing up the place before the aliens have need for it. A related issue is concern as to what would happen to us if aliens were to relocate here. Our planet is already overpopulated.

It would take eons for a change in a dying sun's energy output to have a significant effect. Our sun is in the process of dying too. In about a billion years it will have progressed along the path of becoming a red giant to the point that the earth's oceans will boil off. Perhaps some other more urgent calamity could be prompting the aliens to seek a new refuge.

A somewhat popular theme of some horror movies, and this is a wild one, is that some of the creature types visiting here are looking for fat, dumb, and happy wild stock as a source of food to toss on the grill: us! I think we can categorically rule this one out.

If the extraterrestrials' purpose is really to benefit us, a looming condition needing alien intervention might be the issue of climate change. If the prognosis is correct for substantial rise in the average global temperature caused by human activity over the next fifty years, mankind could be heading for real trouble. Alarming projections have been made for loss of ocean frontage caused by the rise in seawater due to melting of polar ice. New York City could become the Venice of North America. More frequent and severe tropical storms and the reduction in viable crop-growing regions have been predicted. Mister Alien, if you're listening, we could use some help here.

Alien Menace

The biggest realistic cause for concern regarding alien visitation is the public's reaction to finding out that a vastly superior extra-worldly society has been checking us out. Concern has been expressed for widespread panic at the realization. While that might have been a possibility a few decades ago (for example, the terror caused by the 1938 Halloween evening radio dramatization of H. G. Wells's *War of the Worlds*), with all the now-commonplace dialogue in the media about UFOs and aliens, universal panic would seem to be much less likely. This is particularly true for the growing segment of the population that is convinced that aliens have already been here. Earthly governments, however, have good reason to worry in that knowledge of a higher authority with the advanced capabilities exhibited by visiting entities would most certainly erode their influence. Aliens have been exploring here for a long time and—except for an occasional abduction that, for the subject, would certainly be traumatic—nothing of major untoward consequence has happened. A few alien saucers up against our admittedly inferior military probably wouldn't be very effective in subjugating the entirety of Earth's masses. It would take a bunch of them, and to what purpose? If they meant us harm, we'd probably know by now.

Alien Message

Another purported reason for alien contact in many documented cases of human abduction is to disseminate an important alien message. In these accounts, the abductee is supposedly uniquely positioned in some way to assist in getting the word out. Often the theme is promotion of love and tolerance amongst the human masses, with alien guidance toward that enlightenment. What I find particularly weird about this scenario is twofold: First is my doubt that the aliens I met possessed *any* understanding of the concept of love. Secondly, an abductee's memory of an encounter is often reportedly repressed by the aliens. It follows that the message would thus be hidden deep in the person's subconscious, requiring hypnotic regression to pry it out. Those messengers without benefit of a hypnotist would never fulfill their mission. More damning is the fact that people who are conscious of their message and are willing to talk are at the risk of being accused of fabrication or worse of being crazy. Careers and relationships would be at great risk.

Surgery and Hybrids

Accounts have been written of male and female abductees who have undergone surgical procedures involving their reproductive organs, specifically the harvesting of sperm and eggs. Curiosity could be a reason, particularly in the case of the Grays at least, who lack reproductive organs and might find ours interesting. Another theme propounded is that of establishing a race of alien/human hybrids. The idea here would be to produce superior beings who would accelerate mankind's evolution toward the aliens' intellect and mastery of the cosmos. With the proper genetic manipulation, a hybrid would presumably possess the necessary physical, mental, and technological attributes. It has been suggested that a hybrid race would also propel us toward the aliens' supposed superior level of civility and brotherly love. (From my experience, the Grays possess little of both attributes.) Why any of this would be desirable is a good question. Is this hybrid race supposed to be turned loose to interbreed with humans and eventually populate our planet? Or do the aliens see some desirable virtue in our makeup to adopt that's lacking in theirs? (I could point out a few.) And it's quite troubling that we wouldn't seem to have much say in the matter. That being the case, the concepts of free will and freedom of choice appear to be attributes the Grays of my acquaintance need to acquire.

A Gray-human hybrid conceived in the usual way would of course be out of the question due to the aliens' inability to reproduce. Gene splicing might do the trick. But what would be the utility of a human-Gray hybrid anyway? The Grays' characteristics are focused on their mission and they seem so emotionally barren that a Grayman or a Humegray would almost certainly be an evolutionary setback.

Levitation

Myth promoted in some reports would have you believe that the aliens are capable of levitation while under the influence of terrestrial gravity. We're led to believe they can float at will from place to place, and that they can even levitate human beings that happen to be under their influence. The Grays I met aren't capable of levitation and, like us, are subject to gravity when visiting here and have to use ramps, stairs, and ladders just as we do.

Closed-Door Policy

Even more egregious is the claim that aliens with their captive or willing human companions can pass through solid walls and closed doors and windows. The supposition here is that they can re-order atomic structure such that atoms of one substance (a biologic) are able to pass unobstructed through the space between atoms of another (a solid such as a wall.) If my guys (Bud, Bert, and Boss) tried it, they'd end up with a bump on the head.

Silence!

People who have been in the proximity of a UFO often describe the sudden onset of an eerie silence. Wind noise, bird sounds, the crunch of footsteps in dry grass or on gravel totally cease. While this is true, it's also the subject of a myth. Sound isn't really squelched; birds continue chirping and grass still crinkles. The person's perception of sound is blocked, as are other senses to some degree. Alien initiation of telepathic communication with the human mind takes up so much of our mental bandwidth that normal sensory stimulation is partially blocked. Hearing is particularly vulnerable. But so also is the sense of feeling that accounts for burns discovered only after the fact by people who unwittingly got too close to a UFO.

Beam Mc Up

The transporter of Star Trek's "Beam me up, Scotty" fame is an interesting fictional concept particularly as applied to transferring a biologic from one place to another. In theory, a machine would first have to tag and map the exact location of every constituent of a human body down to atoms or even particles comprising atoms. Next that data would have to be transmitted unerringly to another machine that assembles an exact copy from an inventory of various nuclear particles; a very sophisticated 3D or maybe a 4D printer if you will. After all that, you'd end up with an original in Saskatoon and a copy in Sheboygan Would the copy have a soul? If it was possible to disassemble the original rather than map its constituents to make a copy, how would it feel to be torn apart atom by atom? And, suffer one static crash or a few dropped bits of data, you could end up with a thumb for a nose. As advanced as the Grays are, they don't have a transporter.

Shape-shifting

Yet another popularly promoted faculty of the aliens is their supposed ability to shape-shift at will. There are two facets of this claim. In one, the alien can morph into an alternate humanoid form, such as a gorgeous human female with all of the physical attributes of the real thing. (That would be a pretty good trick for a Gray.) In a person without the benefit of an implant, the best the aliens can do is telepathically convey mental images of a vaporous quality that no fully alert human would be likely to mistake for the real thing. However, persons having an implant could visualize a much more realistic image that would still be unlikely to be perceived as real. Cases where a human is under the influence of suggestion embedded in a beam of blue light (see "Stun Gun" in chapter 14), the subject might be convinced that an alien has morphed into another form. The entity hasn't changed; he still looks like an alien.

In the second example, an alien is able to cause a given biologic entity to morph into another: a frog into an owl for example. That would be a hoot... ridiculous!

Tune In

Some people wonder why SETI (Search for Extraterrestrial Intelligence) hasn't heard from folks on another world. First, SETI is listening on frequencies believed most likely to be used by an alien society desiring to purposely announce itself, something that the aliens may actually wish to avoid. Second, it's very unlikely that SETI would be able to intercept alien radio signals. If the aliens were talking amongst themselves by radio, they would choose a frequency range much more appropriate to the task than where SETI is listening. Third, an advanced society would probably have developed a better way to communicate than speed-of-light-limited radio or lasers: telepathy or quantum effects, for example. Bottom line: these guys may be talking to one another, but we're probably tuned to the wrong channel.

We, on the other hand, have been inadvertently advertising our existence since the 1940s. Radar, TV, and FM broadcast signals whose frequency is high enough to avoid being trapped by our ionosphere have been blanketing the cosmos for over seventy years. Late 1940s TV shows (*Howdy Doodie; Kukla, Fran and Ollie; The Lone Ranger;* and *The Milton Berle Show*) have by now potentially exposed denizens of solar systems as far away as seventy light-years to our TV-borne culture.

Our TV and FM transmissions are intentionally omnidirectional, which greatly dilutes the power spewed in any given direction. If even nearby civilizations were listening or watching, they probably wouldn't be able to recover the intelligence impressed on our broadcast signals. They would most likely know that what they were detecting wasn't noise or something produced by nature. They should be able to determine at least roughly where the signal was coming from.

Our radar signals and transmissions aimed at distant space probes are focused into powerful and highly directional beams that would be much stronger and more likely to be detected than TV and radio signals. The civilization on the receiving end would have to be directly within the line of sight of the earth and would have to be listening at the fleeting moment the signal panned by their antenna due to the rotation of both planets.

Scientists have expressed opinions on both sides of the issue of the advisability of signaling our presence.

Time Travelers

It has been speculated that humans and the aliens are related. In the strictest sense, this is plausible in that all life-forms terrestrial or galactic must have been created by the same intelligence. The idea that our visitors are time travelers has been promoted by some sources. Speculation has it that the aliens are the embodiment of what we will eventually become, and they've come back in time to keep us from messing up their future. It's also been suggested that the aliens brought the seeds of what ultimately became us to the early barren earth eons ago and they're keeping track of humanity to forestall a crop failure. Most likely, they're just curious explorers.

Warped Concept

To cover the vast distances between things in the universe, alien spacecraft capable of velocities many times faster than the speed of light would be a big asset. On TV and in the movies, Captain Kirk's *Enterprise* is able to breeze through the constellations much faster than the speed of light. In reality, physical law suggests that a mass cannot be accelerated to reach or exceed the speed of light. Some folks believe a way may someday be found to fold (warp, if you will) the fabric of space-time on itself to get from place to place effectively in excess of the speed of light without actually having to travel at that velocity. Other schemes (wormholes in space) have been postulated as a means of circumventing the speed of light limitation. As far as we know, it's all conjecture.

Crop Circles

Crop circles are remarkably complex patterns impressed in crop fields by the process of flattening or cutting grasses and similar plant life to provide detail and contrast. These remarkable artifacts, which mysteriously appear overnight, have been deemed the work of aliens. Unfortunately, we know that there have been out-and-out fakes with the admittedly very creative human perpetrators ultimately fessing up to the deed. But there have also been exquisitely detailed and complex designs discovered in the light of the dawning day that can't be so easily written off. An effort of the magnitude of some of these works of art would be a real challenge to a hoaxer. So, although an alien motive for creating these artistic marvels is a mystery considering their reluctance to blatantly announce their presence, this may not be a myth. It could be that a rowdy bunch of aliens may occasionally defile a wheat field just to show off.

Ancient Sites

Some people believe that ancient archeological sites such as the Egyptian pyramids, Stonehenge, and the Easter Island stone figures are the work of aliens. Each of these treasures involve fabulous and mysterious feats of engineering and construction techniques that challenge our present-day technology to duplicate. Surely if we're unable to fathom the processes involved, the primitive ancients must have had assistance in their endeavor from a more advanced culture. Extraterrestrials bent on currying favor amongst the heathen would fit the bill. One would think that something as extraordinary as aliens working along-side the Egyptians would have at least warranted a scene or two painted on the walls of a burial chamber. Maybe the aliens were bashful.

These three sites involve cutting, carving, and moving vast slabs of stone. It would seem that aliens with their skills in met-allurgy could certainly have come up with a lighter-weight and spiffier material to use in fabricating a memorial. A shiny metal-lic *moai* on Easter Island would certainly have attracted atten-tion.

I'm afraid we're not giving our ancestors their just due. They were probably smarter and more creative than we think and didn't need any extraterrestrial help.

The so-called Nazca Lines in Peru offer an interesting con-trast. Dating from before Columbus sailed for the New World and located in the Nazca desert in southern Peru, the site com-prises nearly 1,000 square kilometers of geometric shapes and animal images etched into the surface. Created by removing rock to expose lighter-colored sand below, the over 300 geomet-ric designs and 70 representations of animals that include a spi-der, a monkey, and a hummingbird can only be observed from above. The size of the animal depictions is impressive, ranging from around 150 feet to over 300 feet.

It is tempting to ascribe this artistic exhibition to the work of aliens. But why would they create something that only they could observe from their spaceship? A better scenario, if aliens were to be involved, would be the intent of the artists to impress the visitors. An even more likely explanation is a religious offer-ing made to honor or appease a heavenly deity.

Antigravity

As pointed out in "Propulsion" in chapter 12, the concept of an antigravity drive is very compelling. The aliens are assuredly capable of spectacular advances in technology and they've been engaged in the science of spacecraft development for a very long time. It's certainly conceivable that there are second- and even third-generation propulsion systems in use that supersede and outperform antimatter drive.

Even earthbound scientists know how to produce antimatter in admittedly very small quantities; they haven't a clue as to how to produce and control antigravity. In fact, many facets of gravity itself baffle our scientists. Then there's an issue with using element 115 (Moscovium) as the power source. It has an incredibly short half-life of much less than a second. It quickly decays into other elements. Keeping it around long enough to be useful is beyond our present technological grasp. But just because there are holes in our scientists' understanding of gravity and particle physics doesn't necessarily mean that we should preclude the possibility of the aliens having an antigravity propulsion system. So it's probably unfair to declare antigravity drive a myth. All that can be said is the spaceship(s) that I encountered didn't use it.

Abducted by Night

Finally, many of the claims of alien abduction occur in the middle of the night. At first blush it seems reasonable that aliens would exploit the cover of darkness for their clandestine activities. But it is even more likely that in some cases the abductee awoke from a convincing dream, believing that the imagined encounter really happened. This is not to discredit all accounts of nighttime abductions, but to suggest that at times a degree of skepticism is appropriate.

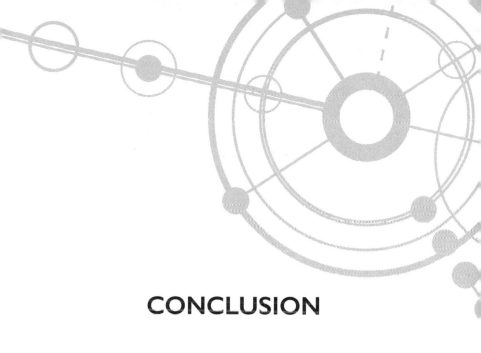

CONCLUSION

My family has habitually avoided discussing my obsession with UFOs and aliens, and in particular my own encounters. My son, who was intensely traumatized during the time the family was forced to move away, often expressed contempt for the subject. He became noticeably agitated at the mention of UFOs on TV and would leave the room. I would occasionally find books I had left on the side stand next to my chair mysteriously stashed on the floor under the table. Ted grudgingly acknowledged my fascination with extraterrestrials and confided to friends that he knew that I believed I had communed with them. He truly thought that ol' Dad was off his rocker. Ted was an ardent nonbeliever.

A few weeks before I hoped to submit this manuscript to the publisher, I got a phone call from Ted who lives out of state with his wife and young son. He was on his cellphone and was obviously quite distressed. "Dad, I've been meaning to call you for a while. I owe you an apology. I don't know why I waited so long because I really need to talk to someone about this! About a month ago while I was loading the boat onto the trailer at the lake..."

To Write to the Author

If you wish to contact the author or would like more information about this book, please write to the author in care of Llewellyn Worldwide Ltd. and we will forward your request. Both the author and publisher appreciate hearing from you and learning of your enjoyment of this book and how it has helped you. Llewellyn Worldwide Ltd. cannot guarantee that every letter written to the author can be answered, but all will be forwarded. Please write to:

Stewart W. Bench
% Llewellyn Worldwide
2143 Wooddale Drive
Woodbury, MN 55125-2989
Please enclose a self-addressed stamped envelope for reply,
or $1.00 to cover costs. If outside the U.S.A., enclose
an international postal reply coupon.

Many of Llewellyn's authors have websites with additional information and resources. For more information, please visit our website at http://www.llewellyn.com.